30 Days with Ruth

A devotional journey with the loyal widow

T0350617

Emily Owen

Authentic

First published 2021 by Authentic Media Limited,
PO Box 6326, Bletchley, Milton Keynes, MK1 9GG.
authenticmedia.co.uk

British Library Cataloguing in Publication Data
A catalogue record for this book is available from the British Library.
ISBN: 978-1-78893-179-3
978-1-78893-180-9 (e-book)

Printed and bound by Bell and Bain Ltd, Glasgow

for my grandma

Philippians 4:4

Other books by Emily Owen:

30 Days with Mary
A devotional journey with the mother of God

30 Days with Elijah
A devotional journey with the prophet

30 Days with John
A devotional journey with the disciple

30 Days with Esther
A devotional journey with the queen

30 Days with David
A devotional journey with the shepherd boy

God's Calling Cards
Personal reminders of his presence with us

The Power of Seven
49 devotional reflections, 7 biblical themes, Genesis to Revelation

You can read more about Emily and her books
at:
www.emily-owen.co.uk
facebook.com/EmilyOwenAuthor/
or
twitter.com/EmilyOwenAuthor

Acknowledgements

Thank you to everyone who, having read other books in the *30 Days* Series, asked for more.

Thank you to my mum, as ever, for unfailing support.

And thank you to God.
Always.

Introduction

Ruth 1:1:
'There was a famine . . .'

The famine didn't last forever, yet without it, Ruth would not have become part of the greatest story in history.
Ruth became Jesus' many times great-grandma (see Matthew 1).

Ruth means 'compassionate friend'.
Her story is one of faithfulness in friendship.

Ecclesiastes 4:9,10:
'Two are better than one . . . if either of them falls down, one can help the other up.'

Ruth's story is one of good times, and bad times.
Sad times, and happy times.
Worrying times, and peaceful times.

Ruth's is a story is of finding belonging.
It is a story of discovering that, in God, there is a place of safety.

Exodus 19:4:
[God says:] 'I carried you on eagles' wings and brought you to myself.'

Each day's reading ends with 'Ruth's Reminder'. This is a thought or a challenge to keep in mind, to encourage or help you as you live each day. It is followed by 'My response', where you may record your journey and reflections.

As you travel with Ruth, I pray you experience God's closeness, and find rest for your soul.

Emily

Hosea 2:14,15 (NLT):
*'I will win her back once again.
I will lead her into the desert
and speak tenderly to her there.
I will return her vineyards to her
and transform the Valley of Trouble into a gateway of hope.'*

Day 1

My name is Ruth. I've decided I want to keep a diary, but I'm not sure what to write. I suppose I should just write about my life, although nothing much happens to me. So, here goes. Today, I was told that there is a famine in Bethlehem. It seems strange to think there's a famine close by, when here in Moab, we are fine. We have all the food we need. People are even coming here from Bethlehem, to get away from the famine. I think it must be really hard for them, having to leave their homes. I can't imagine ever leaving Moab.

Famine means a shortage, or lack of something. Times when there's not enough, and things are hard, and we're not sure how much longer we can keep going.

Perhaps today, you are feeling the famine.
Emotionally, or spiritually, or physically, or mentally.
Perhaps you've been giving, giving, giving.
Perhaps you are grieving.
Perhaps you are ill.

Perhaps you are exhausted.
Perhaps you are hungry.
Perhaps you lack contentment.
Or perhaps you don't know; you just know you're
feeling the famine somewhere.

In John 11, Jesus' friend Lazarus dies.
When Jesus arrives in Bethany, where Lazarus lived,
he asks the mourners:
'Where is he? Where have you laid Lazarus' body?'
They reply, 'Come and see, Lord.'

Come and see.
Not, you can't come and look, he's dead, it's a grave,
it's not nice, it's not a good place to be.
Come and see.

Come and see our barren, empty, dead place.
They invite Jesus to see their famine.

Jesus goes,
Jesus sees,
Jesus weeps.
He weeps when he sees their famine.
He feels it himself.

Day 1

'Come and see, Lord.'
Come.
We'll both go.
Come and weep with me.

Psalm 34:18:
'The LORD is close to the broken-hearted . . .'

As you begin this journey with Ruth, ask God to meet
you where you are.
Wherever you are.

Come and see.
Come and see my famine.
Come and see my empty places.

'Come and see, Lord.'
Every day.
Turn to him, the One who longs to nourish you; heart
and soul.

2 Corinthians 9:8:
'And God is able to bless you abundantly . . .'

Father God,

I am feeling the famine.
Empty.
Needing more than I have.
More of you.
Come and see, Lord.
Come into my emptiness.
Come and weep with me.
Please come, in your love,
and your grace,
and your sufficiency,
and fill me again
with you.
Thank you for being able.

Amen

Ruth's Reminder

God can
fill me

My response:

Day 2

I was only about five minutes away from where I live when I saw a woman and two men I'd not seen before. 'They must be the family who moved here from Bethlehem,' I thought. People had told me about them, but no one had told me how good-looking one of the sons was. All I knew was that the woman, who apparently is called Naomi, had just buried her husband. They were in mourning.

Naomi escaped a famine of food, only to find herself experiencing another famine.
Another 'without'.
Life without her husband.
It was one thing on top of another for her.

Let's look at the book of Job:

Job had a good life.
He followed God, he was doing well in his business, he had a family, he enjoyed good health. He was known as the 'greatest man' in the East (Job 1:3).
An impressive list of positives.
And then, bad things struck.

One day, Job had a series of messages in quick succession, informing him that his animals had been stolen, his servants killed, and a house had collapsed, killing all his children.

Job began to feel the famine.
Things had been taken away, and it was hard.
Job's list of positives became:
he followed God, he enjoyed good health.

Then his body was covered in agonizing boils.
One thing on top of another, and another, and another.
The list became:
he followed God.

The book of Job records the difficult things Job went through in more detail, but one thing never slipped from Job's list.
He followed God.

Job's own wife encouraged him to stop holding onto God, yet Job refused.
'Shall we accept good from God,' he said, 'and not trouble?' (Job 2:10).
Shall we say God is God until bad things happen, and then decide that, actually, he's not a God we want after all?
No.

Circumstances change, but God doesn't.
The God we know and follow in good times is the
same God we can know and follow in bad times.

Malachi 3:6:
'I the LORD do not change.'

For Job, 'he followed God' was non-negotiable.
In a life where things were happening to him, things
beyond his control, Job still had a choice.
How to respond to his circumstances.
And Job chose to hold on to God.

Perhaps your life is a list of things happening, things
beyond your control, things you wouldn't choose.
You're feeling famine.
There's one choice that can never be taken away from
you, or made for you: will you hold onto God?

God is God.
Make 'followed God' something that never slips from
your list.
Make it non-negotiable.

Habakkuk 3:17,18:
*'Though the fig tree does not bud
and there are no grapes on the vines,
though the olive crop fails
and the fields produce no food,*

though there are no sheep in the sheepfold
and no cattle in the stalls,
*yet I will rejoice in the L*ORD*,*
I will be joyful in God my Saviour.'

Naomi would have mourned the loss of her hometown; she'd have mourned the loss of her husband. She'd have mourned in her famines. Mourned for what once was, or mourned for what wasn't.

Perhaps you're in mourning, too.
Things have changed. Things haven't changed.
The future you envisaged has changed.
As you mourn, remember who holds your life.
Your days.
Your future.
Hold on to God.
Hold on tightly.
He's with you.
He knows.

Joshua 23:8:
*'Hold fast to the L*ORD *your God'.*

Make that choice: it's yours to make, even in your famine.

When Jesus' friend, Lazarus, died, 'Jesus wept' (John 11:35).

He wept, even though he knew that Lazarus would
come back to life.
He wept, and he mourned.
He'll weep with you.
He'll mourn with you.
Even though
he knows
that one day
you'll live again.

Psalm 30:5:

*'Weeping may stay for the night, but rejoicing comes in
the morning.'*

Father God,

Life is hard.
My hopes and dreams disintegrate.
I don't know how I ended up here.
I'm in mourning, I know I am.
For what I thought would be,
or what I never thought would be,
or what isn't.
Thank you that you weep with me.
Help me hold on to you,
even as you hold me.

Amen

Ruth's Reminder

Hold on to God

My response:

Day 3

I got married! I was the happiest girl alive when I married Kilion, the good-looking one I saw that day, and my friend, Orpah, married his brother. I got on really well with Naomi, too, and we were a happy family for a few years. Then, suddenly, the boys died. Just like that, Orpah and I were widows. We were young, we had no children, our lives still ahead of us, and we were widows.

More mourning. More one thing after another. But this time, there was a crucial difference: Ruth and Orpah had Naomi. They had someone who shared what they were going through, someone who had been there herself. They had support.
Support is important.

Let's look at Moses, Exodus 17:

The Israelites are being attacked by the Amalekite army. Moses, the leader of the Israelites, has a plan. He tells his assistant, Joshua, to choose some people to fight the Amalekites, while Moses himself would go and stand on a hill nearby, with the staff of God in his hands. The staff signified power and authority from God.

Moses took the staff of God with him.
First and foremost, in any situation, there is God.

Psalm 46:1:

'God is our refuge and strength, an ever-present help in trouble.'

Ever present means never absent.
Whatever we go through in life, God is never absent.
He's never missing.
He's ever present in our days, and lives, and challenges.
He never leaves us, not for a single second.
He is our ever-present, never-absent God.

Moses is on a hill, with the staff of God raised up high in his hands, and the Israelites are winning the battle. They are beating the Amalekites. All is well, until the Amalekites begin to win. Moses' arms are getting tired and his hands have slipped down. Realizing this, Moses lifts his hands up again and, as he prays, once more the Israelites are winning. Soon, though, his hands slip down again, and the Amalekites are once more in pole position.
Aaron and Hur notice.
They notice that Moses is struggling.

Do you notice when people are struggling?
Do you have people who will notice when you are struggling?

Galatians 6:2 (NLT):

'Share each other's burdens, and in this way obey the law of Christ.'

Aaron and Hur don't only notice, they do something about it.
They get a stone for Moses to sit on and they stand on either side of him, holding his hands up. In this way, the Israelites are victorious.
The Israelites won because of support.
Without Aaron and Hur supporting Moses' hands, the battle would have been lost.
The Israelite army was triumphant because every person did their bit.
Men who fought. Man who sat on a hillside. Men who supported his tired hands.
Each played their part.

Paul wrote, to the church in Corinth:

1 Corinthians 12:27:

'Now you are the body of Christ, and each one of you is a part of it.'

Maybe you feel like an invisible member of the body of Christ.
Maybe you feel that no one notices you.
Maybe you feel you have no one.
No one who really understands what you're going through, no one who *really* notices you.

Don't forget who the head of the body is.
Jesus.
He's the one who holds it all together
(Colossians 1:17).
And the head of the body notices what's going on elsewhere.

No one understands?

Hebrews 4:15:
'For we do not have a high priest who is unable to feel sympathy for our weaknesses'.

You don't have no one, you have Jesus.

In living with Naomi, day by day, Ruth and Orpah had a constant reminder that they didn't have no one, they had Naomi.
Someone who understood – who had been there herself – was right there with them.

The same is true for you.

Deuteronomy 31:6:
'Be strong and courageous. Do not be afraid or terrified because of them, for the Lord your God goes with you; he will never leave you nor forsake you.'

Father God,

Sometimes I do feel alone.
Even when other people are around,
I feel alone.
No one notices me.
No one sees me.
No one understands.
Thank you that even when I feel alone,
I can know I'm not.
You are with me.
You understand.
And you stay with me.
Always.

Amen

Ruth's Reminder

God is with me

My response:

Day 4

When we were having dinner today, Naomi made an announcement. She'd had news from a friend of hers, back in Bethlehem, and apparently the famine there has ended! Naomi said, 'God has come to the rescue.' Naomi also said she wants to go back to Bethlehem. Orpah and I looked at each other. We knew what we needed to do. The three of us finished dinner, and then began to pack.

Naomi, who had left Bethlehem when things were difficult there, wanted to return when things were good again.
Naomi received news about what God was doing, and it was because of that, that Naomi wanted it for herself.

What about us? Do we tell each other about what God is doing?

Let's look at John 1:

Andrew is a committed follower of John the Baptist. One day, as they are walking along, John suddenly stops and looks back over his shoulder. Andrew turns and looks, too. He's not really sure what John is looking at, other than possibly a man who has just walked past them. But why? Lots of people have walked past and John hasn't even stopped, let alone looked after them. Andrew realizes it's definitely that man when John points after him, and says, 'Look . . .' Andrew obediently looks, then looks questioningly at John, who continues, 'the Lamb of God!' Andrew immediately catches up with Jesus and asks him where he is staying.

'Come with me,' says Jesus, 'and you'll see.'

Come with me.
Words that echo on through Jesus' earthly ministry and beyond.
Reaching to me.
Reaching to you.
Words that say, 'I'm with you.'
Words that say, 'I want to be with you.'
Welcoming words.
Reassuring words.
Comforting words.

Matthew 11:29:

'Take my yoke upon you and learn from me, for I am gentle and humble in heart, and you will find rest for your souls.'

A yoke closely joins two oxen.
The two are together.
'Come with me.'

The two walk together, and work together.
'Come with me.'

The two pause together.
'Come with me.'

'Come with me,' says Jesus, 'and you'll see.'
There are things to see as we journey with Jesus.
Good things.

Jeremiah 29:11:

'"For I know the plans I have for you," declares the LORD, "plans to prosper you and not to harm you, plans to give you hope and a future."'

What will you see as you travel with him?

Andrew goes along with Jesus and sees where he is staying. Andrew stays with Jesus for the day, and then he remembers his brother. His brother has not yet met Jesus, and Andrew knows Jesus is too good to keep to himself! Andrew goes off, finds his brother, and tells him all about Jesus.

And then, we read in verse 42, Andrew 'brought him to Jesus'.
Come with me.
Already, Andrew is following Jesus' example.
Come with me, let's go together.
Who could you say 'Come with me' to?
Come on, let's do this together.

So, together, the brothers go to Jesus. One to meet Jesus for the first time, and one to meet Jesus again.
Keep coming to Jesus.
Never stop.

Andrew's brother was called Simon. When he met Jesus, Jesus changed his name: Simon became Peter.
Peter means 'rock'.

Matthew 16:18:

'And I tell you that you are Peter, and on this rock I will build my church, and the gates of Hades will not over-come it.'

Jesus looked at Simon and saw potential.
Potential nothing could overcome, because God had put it in Peter from the very beginning.

Jeremiah 1:5:

'Before I formed you in the womb I knew [or chose] you.'

Before God made you, he chose you.
Because God chose you, he made you.
And God doesn't make mistakes.
God had a job for Peter, and his plan was put in
motion because Andrew brought Simon to Jesus.

What might God do through you?

1 Corinthians 2:9 (NLT):

'No eye has seen, no ear has heard, and no mind has imagined what God has prepared for those who love him.'

What might God do through you?

He says, 'Come with me, and you'll see.'
Both Naomi and Andrew wanted to be where God
was.
Do you?

Psalm 25:4 (NLT):

'Show me the right path, O LORD; point out the road for me to follow.'

Father God,

When you say 'come with me',
Help me to come.
Sometimes, I want to hold back.
I get comfortable with the life I know.
Help me remember that life is always better with you.
Thank you that you made me because you wanted me to be here.
Help me reach out and take hold of the potential you see in me.

Amen

Ruth's Reminder

Come with me

My response:

Day 5

We set off for Bethlehem. I never thought I'd ever leave Moab, and now here I am with all my worldly possessions, trudging along, leaving my home behind. Bethlehem is not far from Moab, but it feels a long way at the moment. After we'd been travelling a while, Naomi suddenly stopped. Right in the middle of the road. She stood there, looking at the ground. She looked in the direction of Bethlehem and slowly turned her head to look back the way we'd come. Then she said something that cut me to the heart. I can still feel it now. 'Go back.' She was talking to Orpah and me. She meant we should leave her. We said no, but Naomi insisted. She started saying she wouldn't have more sons for us to marry, and that we should go back and marry into other families. I couldn't believe it. We were all sobbing, and then I heard Orpah saying goodbye to Naomi. Orpah was going back. I watched her walking further and further away. Then I hugged Naomi as though I would never let go.

Orpah set off with Naomi, insisted she'd stay, but then something made her change her mind.

Let's look at Matthew 13:

Jesus is talking about farming. Specifically, crop farming. Even more specifically, about one farmer. This farmer is sowing. As he walks along, he scatters seeds either side of him. Some land on good soil. Those will grow. Some land on the path. The birds will eat those seeds before they can do any growing. Some fall on rocky places, without much soil. Those seeds will grow, but then die because they have no root. Some land on thorns. The thorns will choke those plants as they grow.
Then Jesus adds a twist to the story.
The seed, he says, is not just seed. It represents the kingdom message of God.
The places where the seed lands, he says, are not just places. They are you. And you. And you.

The question is, which place are you?
Are you a path? Already in a place where you can't receive God's word? It will bounce off you. You're closed to it.

Hebrews 3:7,8 (NLT):

'Today when you hear his voice, don't harden your hearts.'

Are you rocky places? God's word grows in you, and then things snatch it away. Difficulties, worries, busyness squash God's word from your life and priorities.

Psalm 51:10:

'Create in me a pure heart, O God, and renew a steadfast spirit within me.'

Are you thorns? Trying to hold God's word alongside other things? Perhaps fully committed to neither?

If we allow them to, even good things can take our focus from God and his word.

Revelation 3:15 (NLT):

'I know all the things you do, that you are neither hot nor cold. I wish that you were one or the other!'

Are you fertile soil? Hearing God's word and letting it take root and grow in your life?

Luke 11:28:
'Blessed . . . are those who hear the word of God and obey it.'

Because we have Jesus, the kingdom of God is among us (Luke 17:21).
Do we allow it to flourish?

Orpah was a bit like a rocky place. She'd been determined to stay with Naomi. But then something changed. Perhaps Orpah looked ahead into the unknown she was travelling to and was scared. Perhaps it seemed safer to go back and stick with what she knew. Even though that meant not following Naomi, whom she'd just promised not to leave.

In John 6, lots of people who set out to follow Jesus are turning away. It's too hard. Trusting God with their future is too difficult. It's unknown. And they turn back to what they know.
Jesus looks at those who are left and asks them, 'Do you want to turn back, too? Do you want to go away from me?'
Peter replies, 'Where else would we go? You are the only one who can give us true life.'

We want to stay.
Ruth stayed.

Others may walk away, but you and I can choose to stay.
Rooted in good soil.
I want to stay.

I kneel before the Father, who knows me by name. I pray that out of his glorious riches he will strengthen me with power through his Spirit in my inner being, so that Christ may dwell in my heart through faith. May I, being rooted and established in love, have power to grasp how wide and long and high and deep is the love of Christ, and to know this love that surpasses knowledge – that I may be filled to the measure of all the fullness of God.
(Ephesians 3:14–19, based on NIV)

> *Father God,*
>
> *I want to stay.*
> *Help me,*
> *help my life*
> *be good soil,*
> *where the kingdom of God can flourish.*
> *I want to stay.*
>
> *Amen*

Ruth's Reminder

Be good soil

My response:

Day 6

As I hugged her, Naomi said in my ear, 'Ruth, Orpah is going back to Moab. That's where her people and her gods are. It's where she belongs. Moab is where your gods and people are, too. You go back with Orpah.' And, suddenly, I stopped crying. I pulled back and looked Naomi in the eye. 'Don't ask me to leave you, because I won't do it. I'm coming with you. Your people? They'll be my people. Your God? My God. Only death will separate the two of us, Naomi.' Naomi realized I was serious, and she stopped telling me to go back. And that's why the two of us are still walking to Bethlehem together.

Naomi was worried that sticking with her would be a bad deal for Ruth. Surely Ruth would be better off without her?

Let's look at Luke 5:

Simon Peter has let Jesus borrow his boat. There are so many people wanting to listen to what Jesus has to say that sitting in a boat a little distance from the

shore seemed the best way to enable them all to hear. After Jesus has finished speaking to the crowd, he turns to Simon: 'Come on, let's row out to deeper water, and drop the nets there, and catch some fish.' Simon had been fishing all of the previous night. And he, an experienced fisherman, had caught precisely nothing.
Not one fish.
He looks at Jesus: 'Master, I've been working so hard, yet I've caught nothing.'

Perhaps you feel that way. You work hard, day after day, at doing, or at wishing you had things to do, yet, at the end of each day – or night – you feel empty. You've not achieved anything. It's not worth it. You've caught nothing.

Jesus says to you, 'Come on, let's keep going.'
'Let's.'
Together.
Jesus doesn't send Simon off into deep water by himself. He says, '*Let's* go.'
Jesus doesn't send you off into deep water by yourself.
He says, 'I'm coming with you.'

Day 6

Proverbs 18:24:

'There is a friend who sticks closer than a brother.'

Whether or not your brother or sister or friend is close, Jesus is closer.

Let's.
Simon protests a bit: I've been working hard, I've caught nothing, what's the point . . .
And then comes the crucial 'but'.
'But, because you want me to try again, and because you'll come with me as I do, I'll do it.'

Because you want me to . . .
It doesn't make sense to me, but I'm trusting you.

Psalm 37:5 (NLT):

'Commit everything you do to the Lord. Trust him, and he will help you.'

And so again, after an exhausting night catching nothing, Simon rows his boat out into deep water.
He puts down his nets.
And he catches fish.
So many fish that he has to call other boats over to help.
Simon can hardly believe it.
He looks at the fish, then he looks at Jesus, then he falls to his knees:
'Go away from me, Lord; I am a sinful man' (Luke 5:8).

Simon realizes that he is in the presence of awesomeness and, in light of that, sees his own failings.

I'm a sinful man.

I'm no good.

Go away from me.

You'll be better off without me.

Much as Naomi said to Ruth, 'Go back. You're better off without me.'

Naomi was right, inasmuch as she couldn't provide Ruth with another husband.

But she didn't yet really know Ruth.

Ruth, who would never abandon her.

Ruth 1:16:

'Ruth replied, "Don't urge me to leave you or to turn back from you. Where you go I will go, and where you stay I will stay. Your people will be my people and your God my God."'

Simon was right, inasmuch as he was a sinful man.

But he didn't yet really know Jesus.

Jesus, who would never abandon him.

Jesus, who would one day be accurately accused of eating with sinners (Mark 2:16). Because they are why Jesus came.

He came for the lost.

He came for people who struggle, people who get it wrong, people who mess up, people who feel lacking,

people who don't think they are worth it, people like you, people like me.
People who think,
I'm no good.
You don't really want me, Jesus.
Go away from me.

'Where you go I will go, and where you stay I will stay.'
So we can say with the psalmist:

Psalm 139:9,10:
'If I rise on the wings of the dawn, if I settle on the far side of the sea, even there your hand will guide me, your right hand will hold me fast.'

Father God,

I mess up.
I'm not perfect.
I get things wrong.
And I forget that you know that.
I don't need to hide my failings from you.
You look at them, and say,
'Come on, let's keep going.'
Together.
My heart replies, 'You don't want "together" with me.'
And my heart is wrong.
Where I go, you go.
Thank you.

Amen

Ruth's Reminder

Jesus is with me

My response:

Day 7

We arrived in Bethlehem today. At last! At first, no one took any notice of us. We were just two women. But then someone recognized Naomi. The news spread, and soon the place was buzzing. I didn't realize Naomi was so popular! Everyone wanted to see her, they were all crowding round calling out, 'Naomi! Naomi!' I was really surprised when Naomi said, 'Stop. Don't call me Naomi any more. You should call me Mara. When I went away, I felt full of hope, but now I'm not full. I'm empty. God brought me back empty.' Naomi meant her family had all died. I understand that. I really do. But to be honest, I'm a bit hurt as well. I didn't know Naomi was feeling so miserable. I know I can't replace her blood family, but I'm still here, aren't I?

Naomi means 'pleasant'.
Mara means 'bitter'.
Naomi wanted a name that reflected how she was inside.
And she chose bitter.
What would you call yourself, to reflect how you are inside?
Satisfied? Anxious? Positive? Busy? Regretful?

In Luke 12, Jesus is talking about worry.
He knows worries come.
He knows worries come to you.
And he knows what they are.
Jesus says don't worry about clothes, what you'll do,
what you'll say, how you'll manage.
Don't let these things take over your life.

Luke 12:31 (NLT):

*'Seek the Kingdom of God above all else, and he will give
you everything you need.'*

God will give us all we need.
Trust him.

Luke 12:32:

*'Do not be afraid, little flock, for your Father has been
pleased to give you the kingdom.'*

The kingdom of God.
Life with Jesus.
A gift God delights to give us.
Life.

Worried by famine, Naomi had tried to find life
elsewhere.
How often we do the same.
Things get difficult, and we look elsewhere.

As the younger son did in Luke 15. He was dissatisfied
with life, so he went looking elsewhere.
He went away full. Full of life, full of blessings his
father had given him.
And he came back empty.
Naomi said, 'I went away full, but the LORD has
brought me back empty' (Ruth 1:21).
The younger son thought, 'I know I can't be my
father's son now, but maybe I can be his servant.'
Naomi thought 'I'm not pleasant any more, I'm bitter.'

Both Naomi and the younger son went back.
And, even in their changed states, both were
recognized.
The father ran to meet his son.
Not his servant; his son.
The women called, 'Naomi!'
Not Mara; Naomi.

The book of Genesis tells us that we are made in the
'image of God' (Genesis 1:27).
I'm made in the image of God.
You're made in the image of God.
And nothing can change that.
Not situations, or worries, or leaving.
The image of God is in everyone,
including you.
And the image of God in you is stronger than any
name you or the world can give you.
It's stronger than any thoughts or feelings.

'I'm bitter, but I'm still made in the image of God.'
'I'm happy, and I'm still made in the image of God.'
'I'm damaged, but I'm still made in the image of God.'
'I'm worried, but I'm still made in the image of God.'
'I'm content, and I'm still made in the image of God.'
'I'm struggling, but I'm still made in the image of God.'
'I'm empty, but I'm still made in the image of God.'
Whatever happens, you are always 'still made in the image of God'.

To the son, he wasn't a son any more. Yet his father threw a party to welcome him home.
To Naomi, she wasn't Naomi any more. She didn't feel pleasant. She felt bitter, and empty, and hard inside. She felt Mara.
And people were excited because they saw Naomi. There was still some Naomi in there, even when she thought she was empty.

Maybe when you look at yourself, you see negatives. Things you don't do, things you aren't, things you should be. You feel Mara.
And God looks at you and sees 'Naomi'.
He sees his image.
He sees who he made you to be.

Psalm 139:16 (NLT):

'You saw me before I was born. Every day of my life was recorded in your book. Every moment was laid out before a single day had passed.'

Even in Naomi's emptiness, God stayed with her. God 'has *brought* me back.'
Not God has *sent* me back.
Brought means to go with someone.
God was still with Naomi, even when life was hard.

Isaiah 43:2:

'When you pass through the waters, I will be with you; and when you pass through the rivers, they will not sweep over you.'

'Do not be afraid, little flock . . .'

Father God,

I am a worrier.
I find it hard to let go.
Thank you that you give me your kingdom.
Thank you that you've placed your image in me.
Help me to remember what I truly have,
and who I truly am.
Please bring me back.

Amen

Ruth's Reminder

The image of God is in me

My response:

Day 8

It's a busy time in Bethlehem at the moment because the barley harvest is beginning, but we're settling in fine. Naomi and I get on very well, thankfully. As we were unpacking our belongings today and chatting, Naomi mentioned someone called Boaz, a relative. She said he's a person of some standing, which I think means he is well-respected around here.

What makes someone a 'person of standing' to you?
What makes someone a 'person of standing' to God?

Let's look at 1 Samuel 16:

It's time for the Israelites to have a new king, and it's up to the prophet Samuel to anoint the new king. God tells Samuel to go to a particular family, Jesse's, and when he gets there, God will show Samuel which of Jesse's sons is to be the next king.
Samuel sets off for Jesse's.
Samuel is to go, and when he has, he'll be told the next step.

Much as Ruth went to Bethlehem, not knowing the next step, but trusting it to God.

Psalm 32:8:

'I will instruct you and teach you in the way you should go; I will counsel you with my loving eye on you.'

'I will be your guide,' says God.

We don't need to know everything, because we have a guide.
We don't need to see the end from the beginning.
We can rest in God seeing it all.

Ruth and Samuel both said, in their different ways, that God is God.
More: that God is *their* God.
And that meant trusting him.

Proverbs 3:5,6 (NLT):

'Trust in the LORD with all your heart; do not depend on your own understanding. Seek his will in all you do, and he will show you which path to take.'

What would it mean for you to trust God with all your heart?
Not only to wholeheartedly trust him with the way ahead,
but to trust him with your heart right now?

To trust him with your innermost secrets.
To trust him with the things you hide.
To meet his trustworthiness with trust.
To entrust him with your heart, knowing it's safe to do so.

'Trust in the LORD with all your heart'.

Samuel arrives at Jesse's, sees the eldest son, and just knows he's the next king. He's tall, handsome, strong. Exactly what the nation needs.
'This must be the one,' thinks Samuel.
'No.' It's God, speaking to Samuel.
Answering Samuel's thoughts.
You know my thoughts, Lord?
God says, 'When I look at things, I see differently from you, Samuel. You look at appearance, at how things look on the outside. But I look at hearts.'
The next son comes.
'No,' says God.
'No,' says Samuel.
And the same with the next, and the next, until all seven sons have come to Samuel.

God has said 'no' to each.
Samuel saw all seven sons, and the God who had said 'one of Jesse's sons will be king' said 'no' about each of them.
But Samuel believed God.

Even when he could have thought God had gone
a bit off track, or that Samuel himself must have
mis-heard, he didn't stop believing.
It can be tempting to assume we have mis-heard God
when evidence suggests so. Or when the world's view
ridicules us and goes against God's ways.

'Trust in the LORD with all your heart'.

Samuel believed God.
And he trusted the 'how' to God.

'Jesse, have I seen all of your sons now?'
'Well,' says Jesse, doubtfully. 'There is one more. But
he's just a boy, looking after the sheep.'
Implication: it won't be him you want.
But it is him.
God has chosen David, the shepherd boy, to be the
next king.

Boaz was a person of standing in the area. He was
what people expected a man to be.
And God chose him.
David was a boy of nothing in the area. He was not
what people expected a king to be.
And God chose him.

What makes someone a person of standing to God?

Micah 6:8:

'And what does the L<small>ORD</small> require of you?
To act justly and to love mercy and to walk humbly with
your God.'

Do what's right; even when it means going against
the tide.
Cherish compassion; even when it doesn't come
naturally.
Take every step with God; be reminded that your life
has a Guide.

'act justly . . . love mercy . . . walk humbly with your God.'

Father God,

When I think I know best,
please remind me that I don't.
And that you do.
When I'm scared to trust you,
give me courage to
know you won't reject me.
When I form expectations of myself and others,
show me whether they are in line with your heart.
Help me see as you see,
and to act justly,
loving mercy, as I walk
humbly with you.

Amen

Ruth's Reminder

God will guide me

My response:

Day 9

I've discovered that things are not easy for us here in Bethlehem. Although the famine is over and there is a new harvest, Naomi and I keep running out of food. I realized I'd have to be brave, and today I asked Naomi if she'd let me go into the fields where the harvest was, and pick up any grain that was dropped or left behind by the harvesters. Even as I asked her, I felt dread in my stomach. What if people just told me to get lost? It's not as though I have a connection with anyone. No one knows me.

Ruth and Naomi are in Bethlehem, and they are running out of food. There they are, in the middle of harvest time, running out of food.

Let's look at Luke 10:

Martha has welcomed Jesus into her home. He's right there, in her house. She can see him.
But she begins to lose sight of him.
As she bustles around, checking all her guests have cups of tea and somewhere to sit, she knows Jesus is

there. She can see him if she looks. But the busier she
gets, the less she remembers to look.
Plates need clearing, cups need washing up, busy
busy busy, and Martha forgets to see Jesus.
Then something inside her snaps, and she sees Jesus.
She sees him, but only to complain to him.

There are times when we do turn to Jesus to
complain, to tell him when things go wrong.
And it's right that we do so.
But let's not forget to see him in the good times, too.

Hebrews 12:1,2:

*'Let us run with perseverance the race marked out for
us, fixing our eyes on Jesus, the pioneer and perfecter of
faith.'*

Seeing Jesus every step of our life-race, in good times
as well as bad.

Martha sees Jesus so she can tell him what to do, tell
him how he can help her:
'Jesus, tell my sister to help me! Mary's just sitting
there with you, tell her to give me a hand!'

Do you tell Jesus what to do? Tell him how to fix
things?

When Jesus was about to be arrested and crucified, he prayed (Luke 22:39–46). He didn't want to go through what lay ahead, and he prayed to God that he wouldn't have to. But there was a difference.

Martha said: 'Tell her to do what I say.'

She gave Jesus instructions.

Jesus prayed: 'If you're willing, don't make me go through with this.'

'If you are willing' (v. 42) acknowledges the sovereignty of God.

He's in charge.

'Tell her' doesn't leave space for God's sovereignty.

In all our prayers, as we rightly bring before God all that is on our hearts, all our hopes, sadness, desires and dreams, let's have 'if you are willing' as an umbrella over them all.

Let's follow Jesus' example.

Leave space for his sovereignty.

Ask, don't tell.

Something which Martha forgets.

Martha tells Jesus to help her.

And Jesus says to Martha, 'You are worried and upset' (Luke 10:41).

Jesus knows.

However we are feeling, he knows.

And he doesn't ignore it.

Jesus goes on to say, 'Martha. Your sister has chosen what's better, and I'm not going to take that away from her.'
What had Mary chosen?
She had chosen to actively remember that Jesus was there.
To listen to him. To see him.

Matthew 5:8:
'Blessed are the pure in heart, for they will see God.'

In the midst of all the hubbub, Mary made time for Jesus. Her heart was focused on him.

And Jesus says, 'I'm not going to take that time away from her.'
Martha hadn't chosen anything bad. Caring and doing and looking after people isn't bad. But Jesus reminds her not to let it stop her noticing him.
Ruth and Naomi were focused on their food running out, yet all the time they were surrounded by food. It was there for the taking, and they hadn't noticed.
Martha was focused on doing things for Jesus, and in that doing, she stopped noticing him. He was right there, and she forgot to see him.

Psalm 139:5:
'You hem me in behind and before, and you lay your hand upon me.'

As we go through life, surrounded by Jesus, let's not forget to see him.
To make time for him.
To choose what is better.

John 6:35:

'Jesus declared, "I am the bread of life. Whoever comes to me will never go hungry".'

Surrounded by Jesus.
Living bread.
Let's come.
Let's eat.
So we don't run out of food in the middle of a harvest.

In Matthew 9, Jesus talked about harvest.
He looked at the crowds around him, and he
had compassion on them. He saw that they were
struggling, lost, worried, helpless.
They needed to be brought to him.
They needed to be harvested.

Matthew 9:37,38:

'[Jesus] said to his disciples, "The harvest is plentiful but the workers are few. Ask the Lord of the harvest, therefore, to send out workers into his harvest field."'

Pray. Pray for people who go and tell others about God.
Pray that you'll be one of them.

Acts 1:8 (NLT):

'But you will receive power when the Holy Spirit comes upon you. And you will be my witnesses, telling people about me everywhere – in Jerusalem, throughout Judea, in Samaria, and to the ends of the earth.'

People need bringing to God.
People need to see him.
So that people can choose what is better.

Father God,

You are welcome in my life.
But sometimes, like Martha, I welcome you in and then get busy, and I forget to see you.
I'm spiritually starving, yet you're right there.
I know you're there, but I forget to see you.
It's like I run out of food in the middle of harvest time.
Thank you that you never take your eyes off me.
Whenever I do look to you,
I see you looking straight back.
And your eyes are full of love.
You're always there.

Amen

Ruth's Reminder

See God

My response:

Day 10

I went to a field today, and started to glean. I was so nervous. As I picked up the grain, I decided the best policy was to keep my head down and say nothing. I listened, though. People called to each other, chatting about this and that, when suddenly a particular word caught my attention – 'Boaz'. I wondered if it was the same Boaz Naomi had been talking about before? It could have been; Naomi had mentioned he was a landowner. The more I listened, the more certain I was until I was absolutely sure. When I got home, I told Naomi I'd been working in Boaz's field! I'll never forget how surprised, then pleased, she was.

Let's look at Matthew 26:

Jesus has been captured and is now on trial.
False witness after false witness has come and given so-called evidence against him.
Jesus remains silent.
Eventually, the high priest asks Jesus, 'Aren't you going to answer this? What they are saying about you?'

Jesus remains silent.
When he did answer, briefly, his words led to his
death on the cross.
Just as he knew they would.
Jesus kept the bigger picture in mind.
For him, that was God's salvation plan.
The reason he came to earth.

Luke 19:10 (NLT):
*'For the Son of Man [Jesus] came to seek and save those
who are lost.'*

What does keeping the bigger picture in mind look
like for you?

The bigger picture is God.
Keeping God in mind.

Colossians 3:2:
'Set your minds on things above, not on earthly things.'

Jesus said little.
Ruth said little.
Sometimes, as the saying goes, less is more.

Proverbs 17:27 (NLT):
'A truly wise person uses few words.'

How wise are you?

The book of Proverbs was written by King Solomon. When Solomon became king, God said to him, 'Ask me for anything you like' (see 1 Kings 3:5).
What would you ask for?

Psalm 37:4:

'Take delight in the Lord, and he will give you the desires of your heart.'

Sometimes, we skip over the first part of this verse to the second: God will give me what I want.
But the first part leads into the second. They are each part of the whole.

'Take delight in the Lord . . .'
Delight in God.
Find him, focus on him, worship him, know joy because – no matter what – he's with you.
When we truly delight in the Lord, our hearts align with his.
We want what he wants.
His desires become our own.
'. . . and he will give you the desires of your heart.'

Solomon asked for wisdom. He looked at the huge task before him, numerous people to govern, and he felt inadequate. He didn't know how he was going to carry out this role. And he asked for wisdom.

Specifically, a 'discerning heart' to 'distinguish between right and wrong' (1 Kings 3:9).
A discerning heart.
A heart that didn't let the mouth leap ahead.
A wise heart.
And God gave it to him.

Later, Solomon wrote, in the book of Proverbs:

Proverbs 9:10:
'The fear of the LORD is the beginning of wisdom.'

The fear of the Lord means acknowledging that God is God. Respecting him. Trusting in him.
Solomon wrote that acknowledging God is God was the beginning of wisdom.
Yes, he asked for more, but God had placed within him a desire to ask.
The fear of the Lord.

What has God placed on your heart?
What would you ask for?
Bring it before him.
And, as you do, keep your mind set on things above.
Focus on heaven.
God.
His kingdom.
How he asks you to live.
The bigger picture.

Philippians 4:8:

'Whatever is true, whatever is noble, whatever is right, whatever is pure, whatever is lovely, whatever is admirable – if anything is excellent or praiseworthy – think about such things.'

Think.
Think before you speak.
A truly wise person uses few words.

Father God,

Help me to think before I speak,
and to look to you to guide my thoughts.
I want to keep your bigger picture in mind.
Sometimes, decisions I face overwhelm me.
Please give me wisdom.
Thank you that I don't make these decisions alone.
You are with me.

Amen

Ruth's Reminder

Look for God's
bigger picture

My response:

Day 11

Boaz was in the fields today! I heard him calling to the harvesters, 'The Lord be with you!' They replied, 'The Lord bless you!' Then I heard Boaz asking the boss who I was. I couldn't help looking away. I wanted to hide. The boss explained I was from Moab, had come here with Naomi, and had asked if I could glean in the fields.

Boaz greets his workers. In Bible times, different greetings were used for many occasions: birth, marriage, dining, wearing new clothes. Each situation had its own greeting.

Here, the workers reply, 'The LORD bless you' (Ruth 2:4). 'Bless' means to wish favour on, to bestow good things upon.
What if we tried it? What if we pray God's blessings on people we meet?

Including those who annoy us, or wrong us, or mistreat us?

Numbers 6:24–26:

*'The LORD bless you and keep you; the LORD make his face shine on you
and be gracious to you; the LORD turn his face towards you and give you peace.'*

As we pray blessing on people, we might find our attitudes towards them, especially those we find difficult, softening.

One of the common biblical greetings was 'God be gracious to you' (see Genesis 43:29).
In other words, *may you know the grace that comes from God*.

Let's look at Paul, 2 Corinthians 12:

Paul, who used to hate everything to do with Jesus, is now a follower of Jesus. An enthusiastic follower. One who wants others to follow Jesus too. Paul travels about, spreading the good news, often causing hardships for himself in the process.
Paul has been tortured, mocked, rejected for his faith, and yet he holds on to God.
You might say he's a 'good Christian'.
Yet Paul has a struggle. He has difficulty. He has pain. We don't know what it was. Perhaps it was to do with sight loss, but we don't know. All we know is that Paul called it his 'thorn in [the] flesh' (v. 7).

Thorns hurt.

Sometimes, life hurts. We can't express that hurt, but it hurts.

Paul knew pain that made life hurt.

He begged God to take it away.

And God said, 'No.'

In that 'no' Paul discovered something beautiful.

A 'but'.

God didn't say no and then walk off, leaving Paul to struggle alone.

Just as God doesn't leave you to struggle alone.

Paul wrote: 'But he said to me . . .'

God answered. He 'said'.

He was there with Paul, in his hurt.

God never left him.

Just as God never leaves you.

2 Corinthians 12:9:

'But he said to me, "My grace is sufficient for you, for my power is made perfect in weakness."'

God's grace is enough. It's enough to get you through today, the next hour, the next minute.

And, as we allow his grace into our weaknesses, as we say to him 'I can't do this' and hear him whisper back 'no, but *we* can', his power is perfected in us.

Isn't that amazing?

The weaker we are, the more of his power can come in.
When we can't, he can.
And he does.

Paul concluded: 'when I am weak, then I am strong' (v. 10).
Feeling weak? Overwhelmed? That you can't do things?
Then you are strong.

As well as hearing Boaz greet his workers, Ruth hears him asking about her.
'Who's that?'

What if someone were to ask you 'who's that?' about Jesus?
Who is Jesus to you?
What would you tell them about him?
The boss knew about Ruth, so was able to tell Boaz who she was and why she was there.
Could you tell someone who Jesus is, and why he is in your life?

What if someone asked Jesus 'who's that?' about you?
What would he say?
He would say,
'Him/her? That's my beloved.'

Isaiah 43:4:
'You are precious and honoured in my sight . . . I love you'.

Father God,

Thank you that you know me.
You know my struggles, my fears, my insecurities,
and yet you never look away.
Your grace is sufficient.
I do find it hard to be weak.
Help me truly understand what it means to echo
'when I am weak, then I am strong'.
Thank you for loving me.
So much.

Amen

Ruth's Reminder

I am precious to God

My response:

Day 12

The boss also told Boaz I'd been working hard, and had only had one little rest in the shelter all morning. I really appreciated him saying that. He didn't have to give me credit, but he did.

Ruth was given credit for what she did because someone had noticed.
How good are we at noticing what others do, and giving them credit?
Saying thank you.
Showing they are appreciated.

What about the opposite? Apportioning blame is often our default, isn't it?

Let's look at Adam and Eve (Genesis 3):

Eve gets chatting to a serpent. A serpent that is described as craftier than any of the other animals God had made (v. 1). As far as we know, Eve did not know how crafty the serpent was. So she begins to talk with it. And, as she does, she is more and more taken in.

Eve begins by being absolutely sure of what God said.
'There's one tree we can't eat from.'
Then the serpent casts doubt.
'Are you sure? Are you really sure that God said you'll
die if you eat that fruit? If he did, he's wrong. If you eat
that fruit, you'll know more, that's all. You'll be wise.
Look at it; it's beautiful.'
So Eve looks.
And she eats it.
Then Adam eats it.

Later, they hear God walking in the garden, coming to
spend time with them, just like he always does.
Except, this time, there's no Adam to meet him. No
Eve. They are nowhere to be seen.
And God, knowing full well where they are, calls,
'Where are you?' (v. 9).
He wants them to tell him.
He wants them to know that they can tell him.
He's interested enough to ask.
Where are you?
How would you answer?

Where are you?
In a happy place, a sad place, an anxious place . . .?

Where are you?
Adam answers, 'I heard you, but I was scared, because
I've realized I'm naked, so I hid.'

I heard you, but . . . I hid.
I knew you were here, but I hid.
I didn't dare come into your presence.

Where Adam was, was scared.
Maybe where you are is scared.
Did you know you don't have to stay in 'scared'?

Zephaniah 3:17 (NLT):
'For the LORD your God is living among you . . . He will take
delight in you with gladness. With his love, he will calm
all your fears. He will rejoice over you with joyful songs.'

We never need to be scared to come into God's
presence.
With his love, he will calm all your fears.
He will see your fears,
he will calm you,
and he'll do so with love.

Adam and Eve had tried to make clothes for
themselves, to cover their nakedness. In doing so, they
were trying to cover who God made them to be. God
could have made them with clothes on, but he didn't.
They were trying to cover who God made them to be.
Do you? Do you try to hide who you are, to fit in with
what others dictate? Do you cover who God made
you to be?
Who has God made you to be?

Ephesians 2:10 (NLT):

'For we are God's masterpiece. He has created us anew in Christ Jesus, so we can do the good things he planned for us long ago.'

Don't hide God's masterpiece.
Don't hide what God's masterpiece can do.
God has gifted you.
Don't cover his gifts; open them.
Use them for his glory.

John 15:8:

'[Jesus said]: This is to my Father's glory, that you bear much fruit, showing yourselves to be my disciples.'

God asks, 'Have you eaten from the tree I told you not to?'
Adam blames Eve.
Eve blames the serpent.
Apportioning blame.
Neither willing to say, 'Yes, it's me. I was in the wrong.'

What about you? What about me?
We will get things wrong.
Are we gracious enough to admit it when we do?
Or do we try to cover those things over?

God goes on to make clothes for Adam and Eve himself.

Despite the fact they've let him down, he makes them clothes.

He doesn't walk away.

God is a safe place for our weaknesses, and failings, and messing up.

He welcomes us whatever state we are in.

We never need to hide from him.

We can hide *in* him.

Psalm 32:7:

'You are my hiding-place; you will protect me from trouble'.

God is also a safe place for our celebrations, our successes, our achievements.

And, amazingly, he gives us credit!

Let's look at Matthew 25:

A man goes on a journey and, before he leaves, he gives his money to three of his servants.

'I'm trusting you with this,' he says, as he departs.

By the time he comes back, two of the servants have doubled the money he gave them.

And what does the man say?

Well done!

'Well done . . . come and share my happiness.'

The man was happy because the servants had done something with what he gave them, and he invited them to be happy, too.

'Well done! You did a good job.'

When we use and live the gifts and talents God gives us, he's happy.
He says, 'Well done!'
He says, 'Let's be happy about this together.'
Will you allow yourself to share his pleasure in you?
'Come and share my happiness.'

Ruth's boss told Boaz about her morning. He was pleased with her work. She'd been working hard, and that wasn't diminished by her having a rest.
A rest in the shelter.
The boss encouraged Ruth to rest.
God encourages us to rest.
He allows us to rest, even if we find it hard to allow rest to ourselves.
He wants us to rest.

Psalm 91:1 (NLT):
'Those who live in the shelter of the Most High will find rest in the shadow of the Almighty.'

Living in the shelter of the Most High God. Protected by him, everywhere we go.
Sitting at home? You're sheltered by God. You can find rest for your soul.
At work? You're sheltered by God. You can find rest for your soul.

In a difficult situation? You're sheltered by God. You can find rest for your soul.
Having a good day? You're sheltered by God. You can find rest for your soul.
Awake in the night? You're sheltered by God. You can find rest for your soul.

'Find rest in the shadow of the Almighty.'

Father God,

I don't feel like a masterpiece.
It doesn't feel right to think of myself as that.
But I'm daring to believe that you see me that way.
Or I'm trying.
And I'm daring to believe I give you pleasure.
Or I'm trying.
I'm sharing your happiness as I use the gifts you've given me.
Or I'm trying.
Help me to keep trying and, as I do, to
move beyond trying and truly embrace
all you made me to be.
Thank you that you're safe.
You're my hiding place.
I'm sheltered.

Amen

Ruth's Reminder

Share God's
happiness

My response:

Day 13

Boaz said I could carry on gleaning in his fields! And all because the boss introduced me to him. He didn't only say I could stay, he said I needn't go and work anywhere else. I could work alongside his servant girls, and he said he'd told the rest of his staff not to harm me.

The boss introduced Ruth to Boaz, and so Ruth could stay in Boaz' field.

Let's look at Acts 9:

No one hates Jesus-followers more than Saul. He can't stand them, and persecutes them with all his strength.
Then he meets Jesus, and everything changes.

What about you? Are you and your life different, because you've met Jesus?

2 Corinthians 5:17:
'Therefore, if anyone is in Christ, the new creation has come: the old has gone, the new is here!'

Jesus makes a difference, a difference for the better. Are you experiencing difference for the better because you belong to him?

Saul now follows Jesus as wholeheartedly as he once denied him.
By a roundabout route, in which he narrowly escapes with his life because he was telling people about Jesus, Saul arrives in Jerusalem.
First thing he does when he gets there? He tries to join the disciples, other people who follow Jesus.

It's a good idea. Find people who share his faith and beliefs, who he could share with and who would support him.
He could expect a welcome, couldn't he?
No.

The disciples in Jerusalem are afraid of Saul. They know that not so long ago he was murdering Christians, simply for being Christians.
The disciples don't believe Saul is *really* a follower of Jesus now.
They don't know he's changed.

Enter Barnabas.
'Son of Encouragement'.
Verse 27 tells us that 'Barnabas . . . brought him [Saul] to the apostles'.

Saul may have been nervous about going back to people who had rejected him, but Barnabas said, 'Come on, let's go together.'

Ecclesiastes 4:9,10 (NLT):
'Two people are better off than one, for they can help each other succeed. If one person falls, the other can reach out and help. But someone who falls alone is in real trouble.'

When they got there, Barnabas told the disciples Saul's story, about how he met Jesus.
Unlike the other disciples, Barnabas had taken time to get to know Saul, to hear his story, to listen to him.
Much as Ruth's boss had taken time to observe Ruth.

What about us? Do we take time to really know people? Time to include them, to welcome them, to value them, to be interested in them?

Because of Barnabas's recommendation, Saul is welcomed.
Because of the boss's recommendation, Boaz welcomes Ruth.
In fact, he tells her to stay working in his fields, and that he'd make sure she was safe.

Stay with me. I'll look after you. You don't need to go elsewhere.

Sometimes, it can be tempting to look elsewhere. We saw that with the younger son in Luke 15.
Boaz couldn't force Ruth to stay. He invited her to, and put things in place that showed he cared and would like her to stay, but he couldn't force her.

We have a God who invites us to stay with him, who cares about us, who would like us to stay.
A God who says, 'Stay with me. I'll look after you. You don't need to go elsewhere.'
But he doesn't force us to stay.

Joshua, who led the people of Israel, issued them with a challenge (Joshua 24:1–28). Basically, he said 'You've got to decide. Are you following God or not?'

Why did Joshua give them this challenge? After all, weren't they God's special people, his chosen nation? Well yes, they were. But that didn't stop them moaning, turning their backs on God, wishing they'd not been born, looking elsewhere.
What about you?

1 Peter 2:9:
'You are a chosen people, a royal priesthood, a holy nation, God's special possession.'

Does knowing you're chosen by God stop you from looking elsewhere? Or do you still turn to other things to find satisfaction?

Joshua continued: 'If serving the Lord seems undesirable to you, then choose for yourselves this day whom you will serve . . . But as for me and my household, we will serve the Lord' (v. 15).

Choose today:
Today, I'm staying with the Lord.
Choose when tomorrow is today:
Today, I'm staying with the Lord.
And the next 'today'.
And the next . . .

Psalm 27:4:
'One thing I ask from the Lord, this only do I seek: that I may dwell in the house of the Lord all the days of my life.'

Let's not be people who find staying with God undesirable. Because it's not.
Let's be people who find staying with God desirable. Because it is.

Day 13

Psalm 16:11:

'You make known to me the path of life; you will fill me with joy in your presence, with eternal pleasures at your right hand.'

Father God,

May I be someone who introduces you to others.
By the way I live,
in what I do,
in what I say,
may I constantly give other people glimpses of you.
Staying with you is the best way to live my days.
I know that.
Yet sometimes I find myself trying to find fulfilment elsewhere.
It never works, but I keep trying anyway.
Help me to stay with you today.

Amen

Ruth's Reminder

Live with God
today

My response:

Day 14

Boaz is lovely. He's so thoughtful. He even told me I could go and get a drink whenever I liked. The men fill water jars, I've seen them, though I've never dared help myself to a drink from them! But it's really hot in the fields, and it's thirsty work, so I'm glad Boaz said I can get a drink.

Let's look at John 4:

Jesus needs to travel through Samaria. Jesus is a Jew, and the Samaritans hated Jews, but Jesus goes anyway.

Ephesians 2:14:
'For he himself is our peace, who has made the two groups one and has destroyed the barrier, the dividing wall of hostility'.

In Jesus, we have peace.

It was a hot, tiring journey and, seeing a well, Jesus sat down beside it to rest.

A woman came to the well, to fetch some water. She may well have hesitated when she saw Jesus sitting there, he a Jew, she a Samaritan.

'Excuse me,' calls Jesus. 'Please would you get me a drink of water?'

Jesus asks the woman to do something for him.
Jesus asks you to do something for him.
Jesus asks me to do something for him.

It's incredible, isn't it, to have the privilege of doing things for Jesus.
But maybe you think you don't do much.

Matthew 25:35,36:

'For I was hungry and you gave me something to eat, I was thirsty and you gave me something to drink, I was a stranger and you invited me in, I needed clothes and you clothed me, I was ill and you looked after me, I was in prison and you came to visit me.'

Jesus is speaking here. And he covers everything: hunger, loneliness, in need of practical help, in need of compassion, in trouble.

Matthew 25:37–39:

*'Then the righteous will answer him, "Lord, when did
we see you hungry and feed you, or thirsty and give you
something to drink? When did we see you a stranger and
invite you in, or needing clothes and clothe you? When
did we see you ill or in prison and go to visit you?"'*

Sometimes, we will be able to physically assist people
who need help: offer them food, or company. But
sometimes, for various reasons, we are unable to offer
physical help.
Let's not forget the gift of prayer.
We can pray for people.

1 Thessalonians 5:17:

'Pray continually'.

But when we do these things, aren't we doing them
for people?
We might echo, 'Lord, we've not seen you hungry.
What do you mean, we gave you something to eat?'

Matthew 25:40:

*'Truly I tell you, whatever you did for one of the least of
these brothers and sisters of mine, you did for me.'*

When we help people, in any way at all, Jesus says
thank you.
'Thank you for helping them in their need and hurt.

Thank you for being my hands and feet.'
Jesus feels people's pain and so, when we help others,
we are helping to relieve pain he feels.
Whatever you do for others, you do for Jesus.
'Thank you.'

So, Jesus asks the woman for some water.
And this begins a conversation which leads to talk of
Living Water.
Whoever drinks of the Living Water will never be
thirsty again.

Isaiah 55:1–6:

Come, all you who are thirsty, come to the waters;
and you who have no money, come, buy and eat!
Come, buy wine and milk without money and without
cost.
Why spend money on what is not bread, and your
labour on what does not satisfy?
Listen, listen to me, and eat what is good, and you will
delight in the richest of fare.
Give ear and come to me; listen, that you may live.
I will make an everlasting covenant with you, my faithful
love promised to David . . .
Seek the LORD while he may be found; call on him while
he is near.

The woman can't keep this news to herself. She drops
her water bucket and rushes back to town to tell
people: 'I've met the Messiah!' 'I've met Jesus!'

On another occasion, Jesus is at a religious festival.
He's been teaching in the temple courts. Opinion over
him, and what he says, is divided. Some like it, some
don't.
On the final, most important, day of the festival, once
more Jesus stands in front of the crowds. Once more
his voice rings out:

John 7:37:

'Let anyone who is thirsty come to me and drink.'

Anyone who is thirsty.
Anyone who feels dehydrated from the demands of
life,
or dry from lack of peace,
or stressed from lack of refreshment,
or cracked from lack of replenishment,
or . . .
Anyone who is thirsty.
'Come to me', says Jesus. 'Come and drink.'
Come! Help yourself! Live!

John 7:38:

*'Whoever believes in me, as Scripture has said, rivers of
living water will flow from within them.'*

Come . . .

Father God,

Thank you that you meet all my needs.
I know you do, but sometimes I forget to come and
have them met.
And I struggle on, missing out on your words:
'Come to me and drink.'
I can find life, even in barren places,
but I need to remember to drink your living water.
I need to come.
When I have, when you've filled me to overflowing,
help me share your Living Water,
so others can drink, too.

Amen

Ruth's Reminder

Share the Living
Water

My response:

Day 15

I'm glad Boaz is looking after me, but wonder why he is. I mean, I am a foreigner! Not even one of his own people. Maybe I shouldn't have asked him, but I did. Me and my big mouth. Almost before I could stop them, the words were out: 'Why are you noticing me, and being so kind?'

Ruth wonders, why would Boaz bother with me?
And yet he does.
Perhaps we wonder, why would God bother with me?
And yet he does.

Psalm 115:12:
'The LORD remembers us and will bless us'.

Let's look at John 8:

A woman is standing in front of a group.
She's not there by choice.
The group is made up of a crowd of people who are listening to Jesus. He's teaching them, and they are gathered round in order to hear what he says.

The woman Is dragged into that quiet, intently focused group.
Everyone turns to stare at her. The men who dragged her to Jesus are teachers of the law, and Pharisees; respected people.
All eyes are on the woman.
People further back in the crowd stand on tiptoe, straining to see.
Jesus has been sitting down to teach.
He remains sitting.
The Pharisees, trying to trick him, announce: 'Jesus, this woman has been caught in adultery. The law says we should stone her. What do you have to say about that?'
What does Jesus have to say?
He says nothing.

Proverbs 17:27 (NLT):
'A truly wise person uses few words'.

Saying nothing, Jesus bends over and writes in the dust on the ground with his finger.
They carry on asking: 'What should we do with her?'
Jesus replies, 'Whoever here has never sinned, never done anything wrong, can throw the first stone at her.'
Then he continues to write on the ground.

Jesus gives them space in his presence in which to honestly search their hearts.

It's a good thing to do. Give others – and ourselves – space in which to truly be.

Space, in his loving presence, to search our hearts and souls and minds.

Psalm 43:5:

'Why, my soul, are you downcast? Why so disturbed within me?'

Why?

One by one, the crowd disappears.
They know they've done wrong in their lives.
They know they're not perfect.
Eventually, just two people are left: Jesus and the woman.
Jesus stops writing, and straightens up.
He looks directly at the woman.
'Where is everyone?' he asks her. 'Hasn't anyone thrown a stone at you? No one condemned you?'
'No.'
'I don't condemn you either.'

Perhaps, despite not being condemned by the crowd or by Jesus, the woman felt condemnation towards herself. Perhaps she was furious that she'd been caught, or that she'd committed adultery in the first place, and was condemning and beating herself up for her actions.

Whether she did or didn't feel condemnation towards herself, the beautiful words of Jesus were for her: 'I don't condemn you.'

Psalm 43:5:
'Why, my soul, are you downcast? Why so disturbed within me? Put your hope in God, for I will yet praise him, my Saviour and my God.'

Whatever we do, or think, or feel, or go through, Jesus doesn't condemn us.

Romans 8:1:
'Therefore, there is now no condemnation for those who are in Christ Jesus . . .'

But that doesn't mean we can live how we choose. Jesus says to the woman, 'I don't condemn you. Live in peace now, and leave your life of sin behind you.'

The verse in Romans above is followed by verse 2:

Romans 8:2:
'because through Christ Jesus the law of the Spirit who gives life has set you free from the law of sin and death.'

You've been set free.
Leave your life of sin and striving.
Consciously turn your back on it.

In Jesus, sin has no power over us.
Jesus offers forgiveness, every time.
He loves us that much.

Psalm 103:12–14:

*'As far as the east is from the west, so far has he removed
our transgressions from us.
As a father has compassion on his children, so the LORD
has compassion on those who fear him; for he knows
how we are formed, he remembers that we are dust.'*

He knows we are weak. He knows we will mess up,
again and again. And he says, 'I've made sure that
when you do mess up, it's not forever. It doesn't
need to haunt you, and shadow you, and make you
ashamed.'
On the cross, Jesus said, 'If you're with me,
there's no condemnation.'

He noticed you. He noticed me. He saw all the things
we'd do that are wrong.
And he made sure we would be forgiven. As he died,
he said,
'There's still no condemnation.'

Sin has no power over us.
Forgiveness is stronger than anything we do wrong.

Boaz noticed Ruth. And he made sure she was looked after. He made sure she wouldn't be thirsty.
God notices you.
He notices everything about you.
And he loves you.
Enough to make sure you never need to be unforgiven.

Jeremiah 31:3,4:

'I have loved you with an everlasting love; I have drawn you with unfailing kindness. I will build you up again'.

Father God,

Why?
Why would you love me?
Why would you even notice me?
I don't understand it.
Thank you that I don't need to try to understand,
I just need to accept that
you love me.
That you forgive me.
Help me to make space to search my heart and
in doing so
to find you there.

Amen

Ruth's Reminder

No condemnation

My response:

Day 16

Boaz knows all about me! He knows I left my family and my home to come with Naomi. He knows I've come to live in a different culture. And he blessed me because of it. He said he hopes the Lord will give me good things. 'The Lord' means Israel's God, and Boaz said I'd come to take refuge under God's 'wings'. I remembered I'd told Naomi that her God would be my God. What did Boaz mean, I'd come to take refuge under his wings? My gods were not a place of refuge. Gods being linked with refuge doesn't make sense to me.

Ruth remembers her promise to Naomi: that Naomi's God would be Ruth's God. Ruth has never gone back on that promise. Yet she has more to learn about Naomi's God.

Ephesians 3:16–18:
'I pray that you … may have power … to grasp how wide and long and high and deep is the love of Christ'.

No matter how long we've been following God-in-Christ, we always have more to learn about him.

Ruth needed to learn that Naomi's God was not like other gods.

But perhaps she struggled with new revelations of who God is.

God is a place of refuge? A place of safety? That didn't resonate with the gods she'd followed back in Moab.

Perhaps there are things about God, things you hear others talk about, that don't quite ring true with you. You can see they're true for other people, but they are things you struggle with.

Perhaps that he is trustworthy, or loving, or caring, or . . .

Who is our God?

Exodus 3:14:

'God said to Moses, "I AM WHO I AM. This is what you are to say to the Israelites: 'I AM has sent me to you."'

'I AM WHO I AM'.
Who is I AM?

Jehovah-Jireh: The Lord Who Provides (Genesis 22)
God gives us what we need.

Philippians 4:19:

'And my God will meet all your needs according to the riches of his glory in Christ Jesus.'

Jehovah-Shammah: The Lord is There (Ezekiel 48)
God is present.

Deuteronomy 31:6:

'The LORD your God goes with you; he will never leave you nor forsake you.'

Jehovah-Nissi: The Lord our Banner (Exodus 17)
God is on our side.

Exodus 14:14:

'The LORD will fight for you; you need only to be still.'

Jehovah-Rohi: The Lord is my Shepherd (Psalm 23)
God leads us.

Psalm 23:2,3:

'He makes me lie down in green pastures, he leads me beside quiet waters, he refreshes my soul. He guides me along the right paths for his name's sake.'

Jehovah-Shalom: The Lord is Peace (Judges 6)
God calms our worried hearts.

John 14:27:

'Peace I leave with you; my peace I give you. I do not give to you as the world gives. Do not let your hearts be troubled and do not be afraid.'

Jehovah-Tsidkenu: The Lord our Righteousness
(Jeremiah 23)
God makes us right with him.

2 Corinthians 5:21:

'God made him who had no sin to be sin for us, so that in him we might become the righteousness of God.'

El-Roi: The God who Sees Me (Genesis 16)
God pays attention to us.

1 Peter 3:12:

'For the eyes of the Lord are on the righteous and his ears are attentive to their prayer'.

'I AM WHO I AM'.
That's our God.

Ruth learned that God is a God of refuge.
A place of refuge.
A safe place.

Proverbs 18:10:

'The name of the LORD is a fortified tower; the righteous run to it and are safe.'

Day 16

Be safe, in God.

Psalm 63:7:
'Because you are my help, I sing in the shadow of your wings.'

As we live in the shadow of God's wings, sheltered by him, safe and secure, we can sing.
Whatever the situation, we are covered by God, and that gives us joy.
We can make music in our hearts.
We can sing, even when life is hard.
Because we are safe in God, and nothing can change that.

Psalm 46:1:
'God is our refuge and strength, an ever-present help in trouble.'

Ever-present.
Always there.
Always a refuge.
You're safe.

Father God,

Do I know you?
Help me to know you more.
You're so big, there's always more to know.
Help me to really know that you're my refuge.
A place where I'm safe.
When life is dark,
safe in the refuge of your wings,
may I find the courage to sing.
Even a little.
Because, under your wings,
there is joy.

Amen

Ruth's Reminder

God is my refuge

My response:

Day 17

When Boaz answered me, he released me from a tension deep inside. I hadn't really been aware that I was tense, until he spoke. It wasn't so much what he said, reassuring though that was, it was the way he said it. He spoke kindly to me. I don't even have the standing of one of his servants, yet he spoke kindly to me.

Do we speak kindly?

When writing to the Church in Thessalonica, Paul says

1 Thessalonians 5:11:
'Build each other up, just as in fact you are doing.'

Build each other up.
Appreciate each other. Value each other.
Say 'well done' to each other. Want the best for each other.
Build each other up.
'Actually,' Paul says, 'just keep doing what you're doing.'
Paul had seen how they encouraged each other.

What about us?

Should we build each other up? Yes.

If we just keep doing what we're doing, are we building each other up?

When we look at our lives, do we see encouragers?

What about others? Would they say we are encouraging? Would they say we are kind?

The word Ruth uses for *kindly* has connotations of 'wholehearted' and 'directed towards'.[1]

Ruth recognized that not only was Boaz' kindness genuine, it was *for her*. It was directed straight at her.

As God's kindness is for us, it's directed straight at us:

Psalm 103:11:

'For as high as the heavens are above the earth, so great is his love for those who fear him'.

Let's look at Mark 5:

Jesus is walking along, surrounded by a crowd of people.

They're pressing in around him.

Suddenly, Jesus stops.

The crowd all bump into each other.

'Who touched me?' asks Jesus.

The disciples think it an odd question, since everyone is crowding around and bumping into each other.

They have a fair point.

But Jesus keeps looking around. He wants to see who has touched him. Yes, everyone around him has, but he is looking for someone specific.

He keeps looking, until he sees.

Just as, even in the crowds, he sees you.

In the crowd, there's a woman.

She's been bleeding for twelve years.

She knows she touched Jesus.

She knows that, when she did, the bleeding stopped.

She knows that she did it secretly, because she was scared.

She knows she's an outcast of society.

This woman doesn't want to be noticed.

Perhaps she doesn't think she deserves to be noticed.

Perhaps she wishes that Jesus would stop looking for her.

But he doesn't.

'Who touched me?'

The woman can't hide any more.

And Jesus sees her.

Terrified, no longer able to conceal herself in the crowd, she falls down at Jesus' feet.

From that position – afraid, on the ground, people looming all around her, expecting trouble – the woman looks up at Jesus and tells him what she did.

Mark 5:33:

'Then the woman, knowing what had happened to her, came and fell at his feet and, trembling with fear, told him the whole truth.'

And Jesus doesn't stop seeing her.
Perhaps you feel afraid, low down, crowds pressing in.
Jesus doesn't stop seeing you.

Psalm 14:2:

'The Lord looks down from heaven on all mankind'.

As he looks at the woman, and sees her, Jesus says,
'Daughter . . . Go in peace.'
Such kindness in that word: 'daughter'.
When others looked at her, they saw a woman.
Bleeding. Outcast.
Perhaps she had begun to see the same when she looked at herself.
Outcast. Unwelcome.
When Jesus looked at her, he saw a daughter.
Family.
Included.
Jesus built her up.

Boaz built Ruth up.
When Ruth looked at herself, she saw a foreigner, with few rights.
When Boaz looked at Ruth, he saw someone worthy of kindness.
He spoke kindly to her.
Jesus spoke kindly to the woman.

Maybe when you look at yourself, you see the negatives, the damage, the view others project onto you.
What does Jesus see when he looks at you?
He sees someone precious.
He sees someone who has worth.
He sees you.
You're the apple of his eye (Psalm 17:8).
Go in peace.

John 14:27:

'Peace I leave with you; my peace I give you. I do not give to you as the world gives. Do not let your hearts be troubled and do not be afraid.'

Day 17

Father God,

Thank you for showing me kindness.
Even in the crowds, you look for me.
Every time I look to you, I will
meet your gaze.
Help me to keep looking at you.
And help me to show kindness to others.
Encouraging them.
Building them up.
Seeing them.
Just as you teach me to do.

Amen

Ruth's Reminder

Build others up

My response:

Day 18

Boaz more than spoke kindly to me! He acted kindly, too. When it was mealtime, he invited me to come and join the harvesters, so I sat down with them and we ate together. There was so much food, that even after I'd eaten all I wanted, there was more.

Let's look at Matthew 14:

A crowd of people are waiting for Jesus.
When his boat nears the shore, he sees the crowd.
And he has compassion on them (v. 14).

He has compassion.
When Jesus looks at people, he cares.

1 Peter 5:7:
'Cast all your anxiety on him because he cares for you.'

Jesus is concerned and, more than that, he is interested.
He was interested in what the people in the crowd were going through in their lives.
He's interested in your life.

So often, our default can be to hide anxiety from people, to present a good front, to smile and say 'I'm fine', whether that is true or not.
Because maybe people aren't really interested.
Maybe we can't trust them.
Jesus is not 'people'.
He's definitely interested.
We can definitely trust him.
That's why we can cast our anxieties on him.
We can tell him: this is really hard, and I'm worried.
And we can know that he will listen with interest, compassion, and sharing.

Matthew 11:29:

'Take my yoke upon you and learn from me, for I am gentle and humble in heart, and you will find rest for your souls.'

'Cast all your anxiety . . .'
Tell him.
You can always tell him about anxieties.
But it's your choice.

'Take my yoke upon you . . .'
Jesus says: 'You do it. You take my yoke upon you.
That's all you have to do.
Come close enough to take it.
Close enough to wear it.
Together.
My yoke is there for you, but it's up to you to take it.

And if you do, all the things you carry won't be so heavy.
Because I'm carrying them with you.'
He invites us to let him share our load.
But it's our choice.

At the end of the day, when Jesus has spent time with the crowd, teaching them, healing them, his disciples come up to have a chat:
'Jesus, it's getting late. People will be hungry. Send them away, so they can go and buy food.'
And Jesus replies, 'They don't need to go away.'
They're hungry, and tired, but they don't need to go away.
Whatever 'state' we are in, we never need to go away from Jesus.
Tired, stressed, depressed, confused, hungry . . .
Don't let those things push you away from Jesus.

Matthew 11:28:
'Come to me, all you who are weary and burdened, and I will give you rest.'

'Come to me,' says Jesus.
'You don't need to go away.'

Boaz says to Ruth, 'Come over here.
You're welcome here, where I am, with me.'
Jesus says, 'Come to me.
I want you here.
You're welcome.

I won't send you away.
Come to me.'

The disciples have five loaves of bread and two fish
between them.
And Jesus uses those seven things to feed a crowd of
more than 5,000 people.
With Jesus, there was enough.
No one needed to go away.
With Jesus, there is always enough.
No one needs to go away.
'Come to me,' Jesus says.
'Take my yoke upon you.
You will find rest.'
You will.
Jesus promised.

After everyone had eaten, the disciples gathered up
twelve basketfuls of leftover food.
Jesus had not only provided, he'd provided
abundantly.

John 10:10:

'I have come that they may have life, and have it to the full.'

When Boaz invites Ruth to go and join him, she eats
all she can manage, and there is still some left over.
Boaz, too, provided abundantly.
Generously.

Day 18

1 Timothy 6:18,19:
*'Command them to do good, to be rich in good deeds,
and to be generous and willing to share. In this way they
will lay up treasure for themselves as a firm foundation
for the coming age, so that they may take hold of the life
that is truly life.'*

Abundant life.
There's no need to go away.

Father God,

Thank you that you are interested in me.
I sometimes feel that no one is,
but you are.
You really care about me, enough
to be interested in my life and feelings.
Thank you.
I'm not very good at remembering to wear your
yoke.
I struggle on, and yet
all the time
you are saying, 'Come to me. I'll give you rest.'
Help me to come.
Close enough to wear the yoke together.
And help me to stay.

Amen

Ruth's Reminder

Share my load

My response:

Day 19

I've just discovered that Boaz told his men
to deliberately leave grain for me to pick up!
Normally I follow behind the men in the fields
and pick up what they accidentally drop, but
Boaz wants me to have more. He told them to do it
without making me feel awkward when I picked up
the grain, too. That was really thoughtful of him.

What do we do with what we have?
In asking his men to drop grain they would not
otherwise have dropped, Boaz was essentially taking
from his own store. He was saying, 'Don't bring that
bit of the harvest into my storehouse; give it to her
instead.'
Boaz gave sacrificially.
Less grain for Boaz, but more for Ruth.
Boaz didn't *have* to ask his men to deliberately drop
grain. Had he simply allowed Ruth to collect what was
inadvertently dropped, he'd still have been giving.

Deuteronomy 24:19:

*'When you are harvesting in your field and you over-
look a sheaf, do not go back to get it. Leave it for the
foreigner, the fatherless and the widow, so that the Lord
your God may bless you in all the work of your hands.'*

An overlooked sheaf is one thing. A deliberately 'not
overlooked' sheaf still left behind is quite another.
Boaz was following the laws and principles of the
Israelites, but he took them a step further.
In doing so, he gave sacrificially, generously,
beautifully.

Let's look at John 12:

Mary has some perfume. Some really expensive,
special perfume.
It's worth a year's wages, so it's hard to know how
long she had to save up.
But it's a long time.
A long time of putting money aside, of saying no
to other things, so that she could finally own this
perfume.
It's hers.

One day Jesus comes. He's at Mary's house.
Mary, along with her sister, Martha, is showing
hospitality.

Romans 12:13:
'Share with the Lord's people who are in need. Practise hospitality.'

Jesus is at their table, welcomed and having a meal.
They're showing hospitality.
But suddenly, Mary wants more.
She wants to do more than 'tick the boxes' for Jesus.
She remembers the perfume.
Probably the most valuable thing she owns.
She fetches it, and she pours it on Jesus' feet.
There was no law saying Mary should do that; it flowed from her heart of worship towards Jesus.

John 12:3:
'And the house was filled with the fragrance of the perfume.'

Before Mary poured out the perfume, the house wasn't filled with its scent.
The scent was there, but it was trapped inside the bottle.
No one could smell it.
But then Mary let it out,
and the fragrance filled the house.
The whole house.

If we keep Jesus to ourselves, we're stopping others from knowing him.

He's there inside us, but we're not sharing him.
If, however, by the way we live and the things we say,
we 'let Jesus out', others will know him.
Jesus wants us to let him out . . .

Acts 1:8:

*'But you will receive power when the Holy Spirit
comes on you; and you will be my witnesses in
Jerusalem, and in all Judea and Samaria, and to the
ends of the earth.'*

Mary was criticized for what she did. Her actions were
ridiculed as a waste of money, as the perfume could
have been sold to help the poor.

Mark 14 tells of a similar time where, again, a woman
is criticized for wasting money.
And Jesus says, 'Leave her alone . . . She has done a
beautiful thing to me' (v. 6).
Leave her alone.
Don't criticize her.
In her giving, in her worship of Jesus, Jesus said the
woman had done a beautiful thing.

Will you do 'a beautiful thing'?

Psalm 95:6,7:

'Come, let us bow down in worship, let us kneel before the LORD our Maker;
for he is our God and we are the people of his pasture, the flock under his care.'

There was no need for Mary to give the perfume, yet she did.
There was no need for Boaz to give extra from his harvest, yet he did.
Neither Mary or Boaz held back in their giving.
They gave from their hearts.

Perhaps sometimes it is hard to give.
We like to grip what we've got.
We think we'd better hold on to it, just in case.

Malachi 3:10:

'"Bring the whole tithe into the storehouse, that there may be food in my house. Test me in this," says the LORD Almighty, "and see if I will not throw open the floodgates of heaven and pour out so much blessing that there will not be room enough to store it."'

Everything we have comes from God.
He's given us so much.
Will we trust him enough to share it?

Hebrews 13:16:
*'And do not forget to do good and to share with others,
for with such sacrifices God is pleased.'*

Don't forget . . .

Father God,

Thank you for your generosity.
You give me so much.
Help me to give to others,
even when it hurts.
Even when it means going without.
Even when I'd rather not.
Help me to practise heart-giving.
To open my heart to you,
as Mary and Martha opened their home,
as Mary opened her perfume.
The scent from the uncorked perfume
reached others.
Through my life,
through the opening of my heart,
may others see you.

Amen

Ruth's Reminder

Give wholeheartedly

My response:

Day 20

I worked in the fields until evening, and when I got home, I showed Naomi what I'd gleaned. She couldn't believe it. It was much more than someone would usually glean in a day. Then I showed her my leftovers from lunch, that I'd been too full to eat. Naomi was nearly lost for words, which is not like her! She asked where I'd been working, and she blessed whoever it was who had noticed me and looked after me. 'Naomi,' I said. 'I've been working with Boaz today.'

Let's look at 2 Kings 4:

A woman's husband has just died, leaving her and two sons, and now she's about to lose her boys, too. She goes to Elisha, who she knows is a man of God, and tells him: 'My husband's dead and people are coming to take my boys as slaves.'
She tells Elisha the problem.
She tells him her worries.
And then she stops.

She doesn't tell him how to fix it, or that she knows other people have bigger problems, or that she's sorry to bother him.

No. She tells him the turmoil of her heart.

Proverbs 23:26:
'My son, give me your heart.'

What's on your heart?
Have you tried telling God? Literally telling him, with no proviso?

The Bible encourages lament.
Lament is an expression of grief or sorrow.
If things are difficult,
and life is hurting,
we are invited to lament.
To tell God, 'This is hard,' and hear him offer to share our pain:
'My son/My daughter – give me your heart.
Choose to give me what's on your heart, whatever it looks like.'

The woman tells Elisha her problem, and he responds: 'How can I help you?' (v. 2).
It's a rhetorical question, but it shows Elisha's compassion. Almost wondering aloud to himself, he asks how he can help.
Perhaps it's a question we could ask ourselves.
How can I help in this situation?

Elisha asks the woman what she has in her house.
Her answer? 'I have nothing.'
Maybe, as we lament, as we give God our hurting
hearts, as we look at our lives, we see nothing.
Nothing but missing.
For the woman, the 'missing' she had was her
husband, her belongings, her life.
'I have nothing.'
I miss the things I used to have, and the things I wish
I had.
I have *nothing*.

'I have nothing,' said the woman 'except a small jar of
oil.'
Nothing except.
When we're in an 'I have nothing' place, there's always
an except:
God.
We always have God.
Always.

Elisha tells the woman to collect as many jars as she
can, and pour the oil she has into them.
She does, and the oil keeps flowing until all the jars
are full.
Her 'except' was bigger than she thought!
Just as ours is.

Isaiah 40:12:

'Who has measured the waters in the hollow of his hand, or with the breadth of his hand marked off the heavens? Who has held the dust of the earth in a basket, or weighed the mountains on the scales and the hills in a balance?'

No one has. Except our God.

The woman ran out of jars in which to keep all the oil. Ruth ran out of space to eat all the food Boaz provided for her.

God provided more than they could imagine.

Ephesians 3:20 (NLT):

'Now all glory to God, who is able, through his mighty power at work within us, to accomplish infinitely more than we might ask or think.'

Nothing;
except God.
Paul says, in Philippians 3, that he once thought that keeping the religious laws, and being seen to do so, was really valuable. Then he met Jesus. And now, all he thought important has paled.
He's determined to let nothing be more important than knowing Christ.
He needs nothing;
except Jesus.
Nothing, except.

Father God,

Thank you that you provide for me.
Sometimes I feel so empty,
and lacking,
and worthless.
I have nothing.
Thank you that you stay in my 'nothing'
until I am ready to remember that
I don't have nothing.
I have nothing,
except you.
Please come and fill me.
Fill me to overflowing.

Amen

Ruth's Reminder

I have God

My response:

Day 21

Naomi is thrilled I've been working in Boaz's field. She advised me to stay there, not to look for work anywhere else. She's worried I'll get hurt if I go elsewhere. She was extra pleased because Boaz is a close relative on her husband's side. She said, 'Boaz is being really kind, not only to me but also in memory of my husband.' She was glad to remember Elimelek. I will stay in Boaz's field, working there until the harvests are finished.

Boaz had invited Ruth to stay working in his field, and had told her that he'd look after her; she didn't need to go anywhere else.
Now Naomi affirms that. She reiterates to Ruth: don't look elsewhere, it'll be better if you stay.
Sometimes, when God tells us something or puts something on our hearts, he sends other people to confirm it.

Let's look at Acts 10:

Cornelius, a well-known soldier, has a vision from God. An angel appears to him and tells him to send some of his men to Joppa, to bring Peter back with them. Cornelius obeys; he calls three people (two servants and a wise attendant), tells them everything that happened in his vision, and sends them to Joppa. 'Peter is in a house by the sea.'

Off the three of them go.
As they are travelling, Peter, 63 kilometres away, in Joppa, is on the roof of a house, praying.
As he prays, he becomes hungry.

Acts 10:10:

'He . . . wanted something to eat, and while the meal was being prepared, he fell into a trance.'

Peter sees a large sheet being let down to earth. On the sheet were animals. Lots of them. All kinds of animals, and birds.
'Get up, Peter. Come on. Kill these animals and eat.'
'I don't think so, Lord,' replies Peter. 'They're impure. They're unclean. I've never eaten anything like that in my life!'
'God has made it clean. Don't call them impure.'

Three times that happens.
Eat those animals.
They're impure.
'Do not call anything impure that God has made clean' (v. 15).

Sometimes, as we look at our lives, we see the bad stuff, and it overwhelms us.

1 John 1:7 (NLT):
'But if we are living in the light, as God is in the light, then we have fellowship with each other, and the blood of Jesus, his Son, cleanses us from all sin.'

God has made it clean.

When we live in the light, it doesn't mean we aren't aware of sin, but that the light of God helps us see ourselves and others as he sees us: cleansed and forgiven. And that is stronger than anything else. God makes us clean.
'Do not call anything impure that God has made clean.'

Peter is still thinking about this vision of the sheet, when he receives another instruction from the Spirit: 'Three men are downstairs, looking for you. I've sent them, so don't doubt; go with them.'
Peter goes downstairs. 'It's me you're looking for. Why are you here?'
They explain about Cornelius, and the next day, after spending the night at the house as Peter's guests, they and Peter set off.
Cornelius was waiting for them, and they went straight to his house.

Peter says, 'You know it's against our law for me, a Jew, to visit you, a Gentile. But God showed me that he doesn't exclude anyone, and that I shouldn't, either. So here I am. Why did you send for me?'

No one is excluded by God.
Is anyone excluded by you?

Philippians 2:5:

'In your relationships with one another, have the same mindset as Christ Jesus'.

Genesis 1:27 tells us that every person is made in the image of God.
So look for God's image in every person.
You'll find it if you look.

Peter knows that God doesn't exclude anyone, but he still doesn't know why Cornelius sent for him. So he asks Cornelius,
'Why did you ask me to come?'
And Cornelius answers,
'I sent for you because God told me to.'

God put something on Peter's heart – that no one is excluded from God's grace – and he used Cornelius to confirm it.
Do you have someone who will confirm – or otherwise – what you think God is saying to you?

Sometimes, it might be unexpected people or circumstances God sends our way.
Other times, it might be a close and trusted friend or supporter.
Who would you turn to for spiritual advice?

Naomi told Ruth to stay with Boaz.
Not to look elsewhere.
Because, if she did, she might get hurt.
We need to stay with God.
Don't look elsewhere.
If we do, we'll get hurt.

Joshua 23:8:
'Hold fast to the LORD your God'.

Father God,

Why do I look elsewhere?
You are the place where I'm safe.
Help me to stay.
Thank you for people who help me see you;
people I can trust and turn to for advice.
Help me to have the mind of Christ.
When I look at others, may I remember
that they are
made in your image.

Amen

Ruth's Reminder

Stay with God

My response:

Day 22

Naomi has a plan, and her plan is for me to marry Boaz! Naomi knows that, tonight, Boaz will be winnowing barley on the threshing floor. That means he will be separating wheat kernels from chaff; I learned that from working in the fields. So Naomi told me to put on my best clothes and perfume, and go down to the threshing floor, but to hide until Boaz has finished eating and drinking. When he lies down, I am to go and uncover his feet as an act of submission and lie down there. Then he will tell me what to do. I don't know how Naomi knows all that. It will be a big deal for me to do this. But I remember what I said to Naomi, way back en route to Bethlehem: 'Your people? They'll be my people. Your God? My God. Only death will separate the two of us, Naomi.' I promised to stick with her, and I'm not breaking that promise. So I told Naomi I'll do as she says.

Naomi had a plan. The plan involved Ruth changing from her usual look, putting on her best clothes, and uncovering Boaz' feet. (Boaz would know from this that Ruth was committing herself to him and was looking to marry again.)
Ruth changed her appearance.

Let's look at Samson, Judges 13 – 16:

Manoah and his wife have no children. Then, an angel appears to them, and tells them they are going to have a baby boy.
The boy is never to have his hair cut. Ever. His hair will be a sign that he is a Nazirite, dedicated to God.
They called him Samson.
The child grew up and met a woman he wanted to marry.
Once, on his way to visit her, a lion suddenly appeared and rushed towards him.
He tore the lion apart with his bare hands.
There were more displays of strength to come, including uprooting city gates by lifting them from their foundations.
Samson was strong. God gave him extraordinary strength.
Samson fell in love again, with a woman named Delilah.
The Philistines were Israel's enemies and, therefore, Samson's, too. The leaders of the Philistines go to Delilah and tell her they will pay her to find out the secret behind Samson's great strength.
So Delilah asks Samson his secret. But Samson doesn't tell her the truth.
Three times, Samson gives Delilah false answers to the question of his extraordinary strength.

Judges 16:15:

'Then she said to him, "How can you say, 'I love you,' when you won't confide in me? This is the third time you have made a fool of me and haven't told me the secret of your great strength."'

And Samson finally gives in. He tells her. He's tricked into going against what God – via his parents – had asked of him.
Peer pressure. It's existed ever since Eden.

Genesis 3:6:

'When the woman saw that the fruit of the tree was good for food and pleasing to the eye, and also desirable for gaining wisdom, she took some and ate it. She also gave some to her husband, who was with her, and he ate it.'

Adam ate because Eve ate because the serpent had persuaded her that, actually, God did not know best. So it was better to go against what God had told them.

How about us?
Do we allow the world, which often goes against God's ways, to persuade us away from following God?

Samson told Delilah that it was his hair that ensured his strength, because it had never been cut.
She sneakily cut his hair, and he became weak.

Judges 16:19
'His strength left him.'

Samson allowed Delilah to remove who God made
him to be.
And his strength left him.
Do we allow people, or ourselves, to remove who God
made us to be?
To squash it, or block it, or mock it?

When we try to remove who God made us to be,
when we try to be someone we are not,
the joy we have in God leaves us,
and that joy is our strength (Nehemiah 8:10).
God made us all just as he wanted us to be.
Let's not allow anything or anyone to remove his
creation in us.

1 Corinthians 12:18,27:
*'But in fact God has placed the parts in the body, every
one of them, just as he wanted them to be . . . Now you
are the body of Christ, and each one of you is a part of it.'*

Samson's hair grew back, and with it came his
strength.
When he lived as God made him to live, he was living
at full strength.
Ruth lived as Naomi wanted her to live.
And her clothing reflected that.

She didn't try to hide it.

Disobeying Naomi might have separated them. Ruth had once promised Naomi that only death would separate them, and she kept her promise.

What about our promises to God? Do they fade, or remain strong?

Dressed in the armour of God (Ephesians 6:10–20), we can live as God made us to live.

We can follow him.

But, just as Ruth put on the right clothes, we need to remember to dress in our armour.

Ephesians 6:10,11:

'Finally, be strong in the Lord and in his mighty power. Put on the full armour of God, so that you can take your stand'.

Belt of Truth? Put it on.

Breastplate of Righteousness? Put it on.

Shoes of Peace? Put them on.

Shield of Faith? Pick it up.

Helmet of Salvation? Put it on.

Sword of the Spirit? Hold on to it.

'Be strong in the Lord and in his mighty power.'

Ruth told Naomi, I'll do whatever you say.

No ifs, no buts. Whatever you say, I will do.

Can you say that to God and mean it?
Whatever you say, Lord, I will do.

Ruth uncovered Boaz' feet; a sign of a marriage commitment.
Then she lay down near him.
Ruth made her commitment, and then she lay down.
She was at peace.
When we truly commit our lives to God, we know peace.

Psalm 23:1–3:

'The LORD is my shepherd, I lack nothing. He makes me lie down in green pastures, he leads me beside quiet waters, he refreshes my soul.'

Father God,

Thank you for creating me.
Thank you for wanting to create me.
Help me to live as you created me to live.
Not squashing the real me out.
Not squashing you out.
Wearing my armour,
every day,
so I can be strong,
and joy-full
in you.

Amen

Ruth's Reminder

Put on God's
armour

My response:

Day 23

I did all that Naomi had told me to do. I was lying there quietly, by Boaz's feet as he slept, wearing my best dress, when he suddenly woke up in the middle of the night. He saw me there and said, 'Who's there?' Maybe it was the gloom or the fact I was wearing my best dress, I don't know, but the last thing I'd expected was for him to not even know who I was. I said, 'I'm Ruth. Please spread your cloak over me.'

'Who are you?' asks Boaz (Ruth 3:9).
Ruth, who could perfectly legitimately have expected to be recognized, isn't.
'Who are you?'
Sometimes, we are not recognized.
We are children of God, yet sometimes we are not recognized as such.
And sometimes, we don't recognize ourselves as children of God. We focus on who we think we are, not on who God sees when he looks at us.

Let's look at Moses (Exodus 2 – 4):

Moses, an Israelite, ends up being adopted as a baby by the king of Egypt's daughter.

He is raised as an Egyptian, but never loses sight of who he is: an Israelite.
In life, as we confront much that is contrary to God's values, let's not forget who we are.
We are children of God.

1 John 3:1:

'See what great love the Father has lavished on us, that we should be called children of God! And that is what we are!'

When Moses is older, he is called by God to lead the people of Israel from slavery into freedom.
God looks at Moses and he sees a leader, someone who will guide and care for God's people.
Moses looks at himself, and sees reasons why God must be mistaken.

Exodus 4:10,13:

'Moses said to the LORD, "Pardon your servant, Lord. I have never been eloquent, neither in the past nor since you have spoken to your servant. I am slow of speech and tongue." . . . Moses said, "Pardon your servant, Lord. Please send someone else."'

Moses thinks, 'There's no way I can go and speak to and for God's people.
There's no way I can be who God says I am.'

Maybe you think that.

There's no way you're who God says you are.

What do we find sandwiched between Moses' protests? Verse 11:

> 'The LORD *said to him, "Who gave human beings their mouths? . . . Is it not I, the* LORD?"'

'Moses,' says God, 'who gave you the very thing I'm asking you to use? Do you really think I'd ask you to do something and not equip you to do it?'

When God made Moses, he equipped him with exactly what he would need to live the life God planned for him.

That's why, when God looked at Moses, he didn't see the 'can't's that Moses saw.

God knows Moses. He sees what/who Moses really is.

Moses tells God, 'I am not able to be the person you want me to be.'

God says, 'You are. I know you are. Because I made you.'

Hebrews 13:20,21 (NLT):

'Now may the God of peace . . . equip you with everything good for doing his will.'

Ruth knows exactly who she is.

When Boaz asks, 'Who are you?'

she replies, 'I am your servant Ruth' (Ruth 3:9).

Ruth is very secure in her identity.

What about you?

Colossians 3:12:
'Chosen . . . and dearly loved . . .'

Are you secure in your God-given identity?
Who are you?
I'm God's chosen child, and he loves me very much.

Boaz was Ruth's guardian-redeemer. That's why she went to him.
A guardian-redeemer was a male who had the responsibility, and privilege, of looking out for his relatives who were in need.
God had already placed in Boaz a sense of care towards Ruth. And Boaz had acted on that care. He'd lived out what God had placed within him, as he offered Ruth water, and left grain deliberately, and gave her shelter and protection.
God equips us and places his gifts within us, but unless we act on them, they lie dormant, like unopened birthday presents.

Matthew 5:15,16 (NLT):
'No one lights a lamp and then puts it under a basket. Instead, a lamp is placed on a stand, where it gives light to everyone in the house. In the same way, let your good deeds shine out for all to see, so that everyone will praise your heavenly Father.'

Ruth knew where to turn.
She knew where she'd be safe.

She didn't try elsewhere first, she went straight to Boaz.
Do you know where to turn?

Proverbs 18:10:

'The name of the LORD is a fortified tower; the righteous run to it and are safe.'

Whatever your situation, do you make God your first port of call?
Or do you forget your identity?
Do you look elsewhere?
Focusing on your failings.
Comparing yourself with others.
Do you let yourself, and others, make you question who you are?
Who are you?
Ruth replied, 'I am your servant Ruth.'
Who are you?
Will you reply, 'I am God's child, chosen and loved'?

The book of Revelation talks about how, one day, we will have names known only to us and to Jesus (Revelation 2:17).
He will give us new names.
But maybe we also have names only he and we know right now.
In our living, day by day.
Names the world misses in us.

Names hidden deep inside.
Names that perhaps speak of fear, or exhaustion, or anxiety.
When no one else seems to truly see us, Jesus does.
He knows our deepest inner selves.
And he meets us there.
'The LORD is my shepherd, I lack nothing' (Psalm 23:1).

Philippians 4:13:
'I can do all this through him who gives me strength.'

Father God,

I say 'I can't' a lot, don't I?
I often forget who I am, don't I?
Thank you that you see me deep inside.
Sometimes that is scary, but mostly
it's just precious.
You understand.
It amazes me that you chose me to be your child.
Help me, in my amazement, to remember that it's true.
I am your child.
You do choose me.
You do love me.
You equip me with all I need.
Help me to always turn to you, rather than looking elsewhere.

Amen

Ruth's Reminder

I am God's child

My response:

Day 24

When Boaz realized who I was and what I meant by asking him to spread his cloak over me, he said, 'God bless you, this kindness is even more than the one you showed me earlier.' I wasn't sure what he meant, unless he was talking about my kindness to Naomi. But my heart leapt a bit at his positive response. He must be glad I want to marry him! But then my heart sank. I thought Boaz was the closest relative, and so my guardian-redeemer, but Boaz said there is someone closer. When he said that, I was dismayed. It made me realize even more how much I want to marry Boaz; no one else comes close to him in my eyes. Then I saw a glimmer of hope. Boaz said he'd talk to the other man in the morning and, if the other man did not want to redeem me, Boaz definitely would. Boaz told me to lie there till morning, too.

Boaz realizes who Ruth is and, in that full awareness of who she is, invites her to stay with him.

Let's look at the book of Esther:

Esther has been plucked out of nowhere and is now Queen of Persia. It's an amazing story.

What Esther hasn't told anyone at the palace, is that she is a Jew.

Then the king's right-hand man decides he wants to kill all the Jews and persuades the king to go along with this plan.

Esther's cousin begs her to go to the king and ask him to save the lives of her people.

Esther replies that she can't. Anyone who goes to the king without an invitation will be immediately put to death. Well, unless he holds out his golden sceptre, as a sign of welcome, but there's no guarantee of that.

In the end, though, Esther says, 'OK, I'll go to the king, even though it's against the law.'

She does.

She enters the room, the king sees her,

and the king holds out his golden sceptre.

He's not having her killed.

He invites her to stay.

Esther 5:2:

'When he saw Queen Esther standing in the court, he was pleased with her and held out to her the gold sceptre that was in his hand.'

The king saw Queen Esther. He knew exactly who she was, and he invited her to stay.

Just as Boaz knew who Ruth was and invited her to
stay.
Just as God knows who we are and invites us to stay.
Boaz put his cloak over Ruth.
Stay; you're welcome here.
King Xerxes held out his golden sceptre to Esther.
Stay; you're welcome here.
Jesus opened his arms on the cross for us.
Stay; you're welcome here.

Perhaps there are times when we don't think God will
want us in his presence.
Times when we don't think we're welcome there.
If we're not welcome there, why would he give us joy?

Psalm 16:11:

*'You make known to me the path of life; you will fill me
with joy in your presence, with eternal pleasures at your
right hand.'*

We find joy in his presence.
Whatever our circumstances, if we live in the
presence of God, choosing to be aware of him in
every circumstance, we will find joy.
Joy in every circumstance.
Joy in resting in him.

Exodus 33:14:

'[God said to Moses:] "My Presence will go with you, and I will give you rest."'

Whatever our circumstances, if we live in the presence of God, choosing to be aware of him in every circumstance, we will find rest.
Rest in every circumstance.
Joy brings rest.
Rest brings joy.
Joy-Rest, Rest-joy in him.
Boaz spread his cloak over Ruth. In that moment, as she lay down, accepted and wanted by Boaz, Ruth knew joy-rest and rest-joy.

Psalm 91:1–4:

'Whoever dwells in the shelter of the Most High will rest in the shadow of the Almighty. I will say of the Lord, 'He is my refuge and my fortress, my God, in whom I trust.' Surely he will save you from the fowler's snare and from the deadly pestilence. He will cover you with his feathers, and under his wings you will find refuge.'

Psalm 4:8:

'In peace I will lie down and sleep, for you alone, Lord, make me dwell in safety.'

In peace . . .
God knows me. Inside out. And he invites me to stay.

I will lie down . . .
I will relax with God.
and sleep . . .
I will switch my mind off, giving my anxious thoughts to God, and leaving them with him.
for you alone, Lord . . .
Living in God's presence is where I will know joy.
make me dwell in safety.
Living in God's presence is where I'll know rest.

Father God,

Thank you that you know who I am.
Even when I don't know me,
you do.
You offer me joy, and rest,
yet so often I am not joyful.
I am not at rest.
Help me to remember to accept what you offer and,
in doing so,
truly know joy-rest
and rest-joy.

Amen

Ruth's Reminder

Know joy-rest and
rest-joy

My response:

Day 25

Boaz made sure I left early this morning. He doesn't want anyone to know that a woman went to the threshing floor. Before I left, he told me to hold out my shawl, and then he poured lots of barley in. Almost as much as I could carry! He said he didn't want me going back to Naomi empty-handed. How kind is that?

Boaz knows he and Ruth have not done anything wrong, yet, knowing others might see and come to the wrong conclusion, he ensures that Ruth leaves early.

In 1 Corinthians 8:13, Paul talks about responsibility to others.
He says, if what we eat – or do, or say – causes other people to stumble in their walk with God, let's not eat/drink/say those things: even if they are harmless for us.
God walks alongside everyone. Some say he doesn't, and deny his presence with them, but that doesn't mean he's not there.

Jeremiah 23:23,24:

"'Am I only a God nearby," declares the LORD, "and not a God far away? . . . Do not I fill heaven and earth?"'

So, although Paul is talking about Christians, we could take it further and say, do not cause anyone else to stumble.
Do not make life difficult for others.

Romans 12:18:

'If it is possible, as far as it depends on you, live at peace with everyone.'

'As far as it depends on you.'
You are not responsible for the actions of others, but you do have a choice about your own responses and actions.
'Live at peace with everyone.'
Don't cause others to stumble.

Matthew 5:16:

'Let your light shine before others, that they may see your good deeds and glorify your Father in heaven.'

Be seen to be living God's way.

Acts 1:8:

'But you will receive power when the Holy Spirit comes on you; and you will be my witnesses in Jerusalem, and in all Judea and Samaria, and to the ends of the earth.'

Jesus actually chooses us to be on his team, to tell people about him, to show them the difference he makes in our lives.

Will you live that Jesus may be seen in you?
He's chosen you.
Will you look with Jesus' compassion?
He's chosen you.
Will you walk in ways Jesus would walk?
He's chosen you.
Will you do as Jesus would do?
He's chosen you.
Through you, with you, Jesus can make a difference.
He's chosen you.

'As far as it depends on you, live at peace with everyone.'
'Everyone' includes you.
Live at peace with yourself.
God's chosen you.
You're on his team.

Romans 8:39 (NLT):
'Nothing in all creation will ever be able to separate us from the love of God'.

Boaz asks Ruth to take off her shawl.
She doesn't know why, but she takes it off.
And he fills it with grain.
He makes the empty shawl full.
Take off your shawl, and I will fill it with something good.

What does your shawl look like?
What do you wrap around you?
What do you hold onto, or what holds onto you?
Is there something in your life you'd like to let go?
Take off your shawl, and I will fill it with something good.

Let's look at Mark 10:

A man comes up to Jesus.
The man's shawl is money.
He is rich.
Self-important.
He tells Jesus all about his good life and how he keeps all the commandments. He tells Jesus that what he wants to know is how to have eternal life.

When the man has finished boasting and is waiting expectantly for Jesus' response, Jesus 'looked at him and loved him' (v. 21).
Jesus is about to tell the man what the man is missing, and yet he looks at him and loves him.
The man is not perfect, yet Jesus looks at him – in all his imperfection – and loves him.

Psalm 36:5:

'Your love, LORD, reaches to the heavens, your faithfulness to the skies.'

Jesus looks with love and, from that look of love, he tells the man: 'There is something else. There is something that you're holding on to. You need to let it go.'

Jesus knows when we cling to things.
He knows they get in the way of our freedom to live the life he wants for us.
'Take off your shawl,' says Jesus, 'and I will fill it with something good.'

Mark 10:21:

'"One thing you lack," he said. "Go, sell everything you have and give to the poor, and you will have treasure in heaven. Then come, follow me."'

The man's heart sinks.

Money is his shawl.

Take off your shawl, and I will fill it with something good.

Could he trust Jesus enough to take off his shawl, his security, the things he held on to?

If he did, Jesus would fill it with heavenly treasures.

Life. Eternal life. Heaven. And isn't that what the man wanted?

But money is his shawl.

Clutching his shawl around him, the man turned and walked away from Jesus.

Mark 10:22:

'He went away sad'.

Boaz said to Ruth, 'Take off your shawl.'

She did.

And he filled it with something good.

Don't go away sad.

Take off your shawl, and let God fill it with something good.

Psalm 81:10 (NLT):

'For it was I, the LORD your God, who rescued you from the land of Egypt. Open your mouth wide, and I will fill it with good things.'

30 Days with Ruth

Father God,

Help me to take off my shawl.
I know you'll fill it with good things.
When I clutch it tightly around me,
please unclasp my fingers.
Whatever my shawl looks like,
nothing can separate me from your love.
I know that.
Or I know it in theory.
Help me to truly know it.
Help me live at peace with everyone,
and with myself.
When I'm truly at peace,
in and with you,
I'll be able to take off my shawl,
and you will fill it.

Amen

Ruth's Reminder

Live at peace

My response:

Day 26

When I got home, Naomi was waiting for me. 'What happened?' she asked. 'Tell me!' I told her everything, and I showed her the grain, and told her Boaz hadn't wanted me going home empty-handed. I think she sensed I was in a bit of a whirl, because she told me to wait. Just wait and see what happens. And she assured me that Boaz would talk to the other man today. I hope Naomi is right. Today is going to be a long day, waiting for news.

Ruth told Naomi everything.
In other words, there was nothing that Ruth couldn't tell Naomi.
Naomi knew roughly what Ruth would tell her about, but she didn't know the details.
With God, it's different.
He knows exactly what we might tell him, and he wants to share the details.
Amazing God who wants to be part of every detail in our lives.

Day 26

Psalm 139:1:

*'You have searched me, L*ORD*, and you know me.'*

He knows, yet he invites us to tell him. To link with
him and, as we do, remember we are not alone.
Whatever we tell him, he'll stay.
Nothing scares God away.

Psalm 23:4 (NLT):

*'Even when I walk through the darkest valley, I will not
be afraid, for you are close beside me.'*

In the darkest times, he's there.
David wrote these words after he became king of Israel.
I will not be afraid.
Sometimes, we, too, are in that 'I won't be afraid'
place. We feel brave, and confident, and strong.
And sometimes, we are afraid.
We're scared.
We don't feel brave.
David, who knew the 'I won't be afraid' place, also
knew the 'I'm afraid' place.

Psalm 56:3 (NLT):

'But when I am afraid, I will put my trust in you.'

When I am afraid . . .
The Hebrew word for 'afraid' in these two verses of
David carries the meaning of afraid, and of awesome,
depending on the context.[2]

Perhaps we could apply both together.
I will not be afraid; I have an awesome God with me.
When I am afraid, I have an awesome God with me.
Trust him.

Difficult times will come.
Jesus said so.

John 16:33:
'In this world you will have trouble. But take heart! I have overcome the world.'

Jesus has just been telling his disciples that things were going to be difficult. And he tells them why he has:

John 16:33 (NLT):
'I have told you all this so that you may have peace in me.'

'So
That
You
May
Have
Peace
In
Me.'

You 'may' have peace.
Jesus is giving permission.
When things are overwhelming, he says you have
permission to find peace in it all.
Perhaps we need that permission;
permission to let go and, as we do,
to find peace in him,
even in the 'When I am afraid' times.
When I am afraid, I will trust in you.
I may have peace.
I have permission.

Ruth was in a whirl, not sure what was happening,
head spinning, and Naomi says,
'Wait.'
Just wait.

Isaiah 40:31 (NLT):
'But those who trust in ['wait upon' KJV] the LORD will
find new strength. They will soar high on wings like
eagles. They will run and not grow weary. They will walk
and not faint.'

Take time to wait.
When we wait on the Lord, spending time just sitting
in his presence, he prepares us.

As Ruth waited, she was excited for what lay ahead.
Are we expectant as we wait with the Lord?

Take off your shawl, and let God fill it with something good.
And, just as Ruth showed Naomi the grain in her shawl from Boaz, we'll have blessings and gifts from God to share with others.

Ephesians 1:3:

'Praise be to the God and Father of our Lord Jesus Christ, who has blessed us in the heavenly realms with every spiritual blessing in Christ.'

Father God,

Thank you that, because you know me,
you don't need to learn
anything about me, and yet
you want to share in the details
of my life.
You know when I'm feeling brave.
You know when I'm afraid.
You share those things with me and
over all, you whisper,
'Don't be afraid.
You may have peace.
In me.'

Amen

Ruth's Reminder

I have an awesome
God with me

My response:

Day 27

Naomi was right! Boaz did talk to the other man, and he's just told me about it. Apparently, their conversation went like this:

Boaz: Naomi is selling some land that belonged to her husband. You are first in line to buy it.

(NB I didn't know about this land, but that wasn't uppermost in my mind right then.)

Other Man: OK, I'll buy it.

B: When you do, you'll also get Ruth.

OM: Then I can't, it might make things difficult in my own estate. Buy it yourself.

B: OK.

And that was that!

'I can't . . .'

Let's look at a parable Jesus told in Luke 14:

A man plans a banquet and invites lots of people. When it's time for the party, he asks his servant to go and tell his guests to come.
'Come! Everything is ready for you.'
When the servant gets back, alone, the man says, 'Well? Where is everyone?'

And the servant tells him:
'They're not coming.'
'But why? Everything is ready!'
'They say they can't. They have other things to do.
Things to check on. Things they can't do if they come.'
'What things?'
'Check on a field, or oxen, or their wife.'

They'd been invited, they'd accepted the invitation,
yet when the time came to live the reality of it, they
said, 'I can't'.
Just as the other man said to Boaz, 'I can't.'
I can't live the reality of my position.
In saying 'I can't' the wedding guests were saying no to
a banquet that had been prepared especially for them.
Prepared, because they'd accepted an invitation.
Perhaps we've accepted an invitation. An invitation
from Jesus: 'Can I come into your life?'

Revelation 3:20:

*'Here I am! I stand at the door and knock. If anyone
hears my voice and opens the door, I will come in and
eat with that person, and they with me.'*

We've said 'yes' to Jesus, and he's entered our lives,
but maybe we don't live in the fullness of the life
we've accepted.
I can't.
What do we accept, yet struggle to live in reality?

171

Galatians 5:1:
'It is for freedom that Christ has set us free. Stand firm, then, and do not let yourselves be burdened again by a yoke of slavery.'

Don't be burdened again.
Don't slip back to how you were before.
Jesus has set you free.
I don't experience freedom.
I can't live the reality of my position.

Jesus helps you stand firm.
I attempt to do things in my own strength.
I can't live the reality of my position.

Jesus shares your yoke.
I try to carry my burdens alone.
I can't live the reality of my position.

I'm turning down a banquet that's been especially prepared for me.
Do you really want to turn it down?
Do you really want to say no to it?

1 Corinthians 2:9 (NLT):
'No eye has seen, no ear has heard, and no mind has imagined what God has prepared for those who love him.'

Boaz didn't hesitate. He didn't think, 'If I redeem, perhaps I'll make things difficult in my own estate.'
He thought of Ruth.
Jesus, when he left heaven, didn't hesitate.

Hebrews 12:2:

'For the joy that was set before him he endured the cross, scorning its shame . . .'

Jesus showed contempt for the shame of the cross.
Humiliating though it was, it was nothing compared to the joy he bought through it.
What joy?
You-joy, that's what joy.
Jesus stayed on that cross because of you.
And, as he hung there, he knew he was buying your salvation.
And that gave him joy.
Jesus was the only one who could buy salvation.
Redemption.
Welcoming you.
The only one who didn't need to say, 'I can't.'
Because he could.
He could.
He can.
He does.

Hebrew 12:2:
'. . . and sat down at the right hand of the throne of God.'

Everything is ready.

> *Father God,*
>
> *I do need to check my priorities.*
> *Check what's most important.*
> *When I don't, I risk not living the*
> *reality of my position*
> *as your child.*
> *I risk not living in freedom,*
> *which means I live in captivity.*
> *You offer me freedom, and when*
> *I say 'I can't',*
> *I choose captivity.*
> *Help me to say 'I can'*
> *and find freedom*
> *in you.*
> *You give me so much.*
> *Thank you.*
>
> *Amen*

Ruth's Reminder

Live the reality of
my position

My response:

Day 28

Apparently it wasn't just Boaz and the other man talking. There were other important people – leaders – around while they talked, and Boaz asked them to be witnesses that he had bought all of Elimelek's property. Not only that he'd bought the property, but that he was going to marry me, as well! They agreed, and then they blessed me. Me! They were pleased I was going to be Boaz's wife. Not as pleased as I was, though. We did get married, and it was such a happy day!

Ruth and Boaz get married, and everyone is happy. More than happy. The people who witnessed Boaz winning the right to marry Ruth, blessed her. They blessed Ruth. They wanted her life to be full of good things.
What about us? As we look around at friends, neighbours, colleagues, do we want their lives to be full of good things?
God does!

Day 28

Matthew 7:9–11 (NLT):

'You parents – if your children ask for a loaf of bread, do you give them a stone instead? Or if they ask for a fish, do you give them a snake? Of course not! So if you sinful people know how to give good gifts to your children, how much more will your heavenly Father give good gifts to those who ask him.'

What about when we look at ourselves? Do we think we are worth blessing?

Do you think you are worth blessing?

Perhaps Ruth, a foreigner, wondered why people were blessing her, why they were so happy she was becoming one of them. Perhaps she even wondered if she was worthy of being so blessed.

Let's look at Luke 15:

Ninety-nine. That's how many sheep the man counts. There should be 100. One is not there. But it's only one out of 100. Hardly worth noticing.

That's not how the shepherd sees things.

One sheep is missing.

His flock is incomplete.

The shepherd goes off, and searches high and low until he finds that sheep.

When he gets back, he throws a party.

A rejoicing party.

Luke 15:6:

'Rejoice with me; I have found my lost sheep.'

For a time, the sheep was not part of the rest of the flock, and when it did rejoin, it was celebrated.

Luke 15:7:

[Jesus said]: 'I tell you that in the same way there will be more rejoicing in heaven over one sinner who repents than over ninety-nine righteous people who do not need to repent.'

Heaven celebrates when we repent.
There's a party in heaven when we turn to God.
Every time.

'Rejoice with me; I have found my lost sheep.'
The shepherd was saying, 'I'm happy! Come and be happy with me.'
Do we invite people to rejoice with us?
Sharing our good times.
Do we rejoice with others?
Sharing their good times.

Romans 12:15:

'Rejoice with those who rejoice; mourn with those who mourn.'

Sometimes, people can only mourn with us if we tell them what's going on.

It's our responsibility.
It means being vulnerable, yes, but if we won't, then people can't mourn with us.

Sometimes, we can only rejoice with others by making a deliberate decision to do so.
Perhaps what we are celebrating in their life is something we long for in our own.
Something absent from us, highlighted by its presence with them.

Whether we are mourning or rejoicing, whether it comes easily or not, we can pray God's blessing on the person.
Ask him to bless them.
And, as we do, as we pray his best for them, he works on our hearts, inwardly transforming us, until, one day, we find we mean it.
Heaven invades our hearts, even in our pain, and fills them to overflowing.

Is your life good?
Maybe you think your life is so un-good that nothing could change that.
Leave it to God.
Put yourself in his hands.
Wait for him.
He will bless your life.

Those that blessed Ruth wanted her life to be good.
God blesses your life, because he wants it to be good.

Psalm 103:4,5:
'[The Lord] who redeems your life from the pit and crowns you with love and compassion, who satisfies your desires with good things so that your youth is renewed like the eagle's.'

Father God,

Sometimes, people are missing.
Sometimes, I'm missing.
Thank you that you always look for us,
and bring us back.
Rejoicing and mourning with others
is not always easy.
Letting others rejoice and mourn with me
is even less easy.
Help me dare to be vulnerable.
As I pray your blessing on others
and on myself,
help us to welcome you and each other.

Amen

Ruth's Reminder

Be present with others

My response:

Day 29

We've been married a while now, and we have a baby boy. We called him Obed, which means 'servant'. I will never forget the joy on Naomi's face when she held our baby in her arms. I don't think she'd call herself Mara any more! Her friends all came and rejoiced with her, too. One of them called me 'Naomi's daughter-in-law, who loves her and is better than seven sons.' I was amazed at that. This is me, who arrived as a foreigner, being fully welcomed into my new family and friends.

Ruth gives birth to a baby boy. In those days, having a son was seen as vital. The family line was passed through sons, and it was the role of a son to look after his parents in later life.

Now Ruth has a son. In the eyes of society, she's made it.

Naomi is, of course, delighted with the child.

Her friends share her delight.

These friends may well have been some of the ones who, when Naomi arrived back in Bethlehem, had been told to call her Mara. Bitter.

Yet here they are, praising God with and for her.

And she's letting them.
She's not saying, 'Call me Mara' now.
And they're not calling her Mara.
They were with her in her bitter time, and they
recognize that she's not that person any more.
They allow her to move on.
To change her name back.

To God, Naomi's name never changed.
He didn't call her Mara.
'Pleasant' did not become 'bitter' to him,
no matter how Naomi felt about herself.
However we feel about ourselves, God doesn't
change his mind about us:

Isaiah 43:4:

*'You are precious and honoured in my sight, and . . . I
love you'.*

God doesn't change his mind about us, but that
doesn't mean he ignores how we are feeling.

Not long before his death, Jesus speaks to Peter's 'Mara'.
The person Peter used to be.
Simon.
Jesus tells Simon that Satan is interested in him (in
fact, in all the disciples). So much so, that Satan has
even asked to sift him 'as wheat' (Luke 22:31–34).
Sifting wheat involves beating it and thrashing it.

Satan wanted to give Simon a hard time.
And Jesus acknowledges that.
He doesn't ignore it.
It's going to be difficult for the Simon in Peter.
Jesus continues, 'But . . .'
But a hard time doesn't mean you'll be finished.

Luke 22:32:
'But I have prayed for you, Simon, that your faith may not fail.'

Jesus prayed for Simon.
Jesus prays for you.

Hebrews 7:24,25:
'But because Jesus lives for ever, he has a permanent priesthood. Therefore he is able to save completely those who come to God through him, because he always lives to intercede for them.'

Amazing though it is, Jesus actually prays for each one of us.
You are being prayed for, right this minute.

What did Jesus plead in prayer for Simon?
That Satan wouldn't get to sift him 'as wheat'?
No.
Jesus prayed that Simon's faith would not fail.

When people, or we ourselves, are having difficult
times, we may – understandably – ask God to stop
those times.
Let's not forget to also echo Jesus in it all, and pray
that our/their faith remains firm.

Once, a man told Jesus: 'I do believe, I do. Help me
overcome the bit in me that struggles to hold on to
that belief' (Mark 9:24).

'I have prayed . . . that your faith may not fail.'
Peter's 'Mara' – Simon – is addressed by Jesus.
Simon needed praying for.
Just as Naomi's friends were there with the Mara in
Naomi,
Jesus is there with the Simon in Peter.
Satan wanted Simon.
And Jesus prayed for Simon.
But then Jesus called him Peter again.
'The Rock.'
When Jesus met Simon, he gave him a new name;
a name which overwrote the first,
and nothing could change that.

Romans 8:37–39:

'In all these things we are more than conquerors through him who loved us. For I am convinced that neither death nor life, neither angels nor demons, neither the present nor the future, nor any powers, neither height nor depth, nor anything else in all creation, will be able to separate us from the love of God that is in Christ Jesus our Lord.'

Simon had no lasting power over Peter.
Mara had no lasting power over Naomi.
The person you used to be has no lasting power over the person you are now in Jesus.
Precious, honoured, loved.

The women also point out to Naomi that Ruth is better than seven sons.
That's not what their culture would have held, but the women point it out to Naomi anyway.
What's a 'son' equivalent today? What shows we've 'made it'?
Good job? Good holidays? Good car? Good health? Good intellect? Good ability . . .?
What's a 'Ruth' equivalent today? What's better than all the 'sons' put together?
Jesus.

Paul had lots of 'son' equivalents. In Philippians 3, he lists them. Born into the right family, studied at the

right school, gained the best qualifications, rose to the top in his field . . .
Then Paul meets Jesus. And he realizes that there is something better than all the 'sons' put together. Jesus.

Philippians 3:7–9 (NLT):

'I once thought these things were valuable, but now I consider them worthless because of what Christ has done. Yes, everything else is worthless when compared with the infinite value of knowing Christ Jesus my Lord. For his sake I have discarded everything else, counting it all as garbage, so that I could gain Christ and become one with him. I no longer count on my own righteousness through obeying the law; rather, I become righteous through faith in Christ. For God's way of making us right with himself depends on faith.'

'I have prayed . . . that your faith may not fail', says Jesus.
And Philippians tells us why.
Because God wants us right with him.
Made right with him,
right where he is.
'I have prayed . . .'

'Everything else is worthless when compared with the infinite value of knowing Christ Jesus my Lord', says Paul.
Can you say that?
However good anything in life is, Jesus is better.
However bad anything in life is, Jesus is better.

Ruth, who arrived as a foreigner, now finds herself among family and friends.
Welcomed by them.
Celebrated by them.
One of them.

Ephesians 2:17,18:
'He came and preached peace to you who were far away and peace to those who were near. For through him we both have access to the Father by one Spirit.'

'I have prayed . . . that your faith may not fail.'

Ephesians 2:19,20:
'Consequently, you are no longer foreigners and strangers, but fellow citizens with God's people and also members of his household, built on the foundation of the apostles and prophets, with Christ Jesus himself as the chief cornerstone.'

'I have prayed . . . that your faith may not fail.'

Day 29

Father God,

It's so easy to want to follow the crowd.
Especially when life is hard, it seems
everyone else has it better than me.
And I change my name back to who I was before I
met you.
Thank you that Jesus says to me:
'I have prayed . . . that your faith may not fail.'
Thank you that nothing can separate me from
your love.
Thank you that you don't change my name back,
even when I do.
Help me to be like Paul,
remembering that nothing is ever better
than knowing you.

Amen

Ruth's Reminder

Jesus prays for me

My response:

Day 30

I've just looked back through this diary. I laughed when I saw that I wrote 'nothing much happens to me'. If I ever keep another diary, I won't write that at the beginning. But what really struck me as I looked back was how, at the start, I didn't know God. It's hard to remember not knowing him; he's so much part of my life and days now. He fills me with a peace I didn't know I needed. It's been quite a journey but, as I look to God and know he welcomes me, do you know what? I wouldn't change a thing.

'There's no point in asking me to leave you,' said Ruth to Naomi as Naomi pointed out the reasons Ruth would be better off elsewhere.
In other words, 'Even when life is dark, as it is right now, I'm staying with you.'
We have a God who says the same to us (see Psalm 23:4):

'Even though you walk through the darkest valley – and the valley times will come – don't be scared. I'm with you. Protecting you. Comforting you.'

Ruth said, 'I'm staying with you, Naomi, and your God will be my God, too.'

In following God, Ruth experienced famine.

In the middle of harvest time, she and Naomi ran out of food.

But, crucially, Ruth was blessed through her famine.

Through famine, Ruth learned to look. To lift up her eyes (Psalm 121:1) and realize that she had more than she thought.

Without her famine – and Boaz – perhaps Ruth wouldn't have realized that God provides abundantly.

Luke 6:21:

'Blessed are you who hunger now, for you will be satisfied.
Blessed are you who weep now, for you will laugh.'

In our famine times, those times when we run out, God is there.

When we feel empty, God is still with us.

Let's look to him, even through our tears, through our pain, through our bewilderment, through our lacking.

Jehovah-Shammah: The Lord is There.

Abundantly here.

And one day, as the book of Revelation tells us, he will wipe our tears away.

Forever.

1 Peter 3:10,11:
'Whoever would love life and see good days . . . must seek peace and pursue it.'

How do we seek peace?
Perhaps one way is to echo the mourners at the grave of Lazarus:
'Come and see, Lord' (John 11:34).
Come and see.

As we've journeyed with Ruth, we've been inviting Jesus into our lives, inviting him to 'come and see' the famine times and the full times, and asking him to be present in them.
'Take off your shawl,' says Jesus, 'and let me fill it with something good.
Let me fill you with me.'

Ephesians 2:14:
'For he himself is our peace.'

Keep coming, Lord; keep seeing.

'Ruth' means compassionate friend.
She stuck with Naomi.
'Where you go, I'll go.'
Ruth proved it. She lived what she said. She lived the reality of her name.

Ruth was there, caring and sharing, when Naomi was in a Mara place. Bitter.
And she was there, caring and sharing, when Naomi was in a Naomi place. Pleasant.

Ruth 1:16,17 (NLT):

*'But Ruth replied, "Don't ask me to leave you and turn back. Wherever you go, I will go; wherever you live, I will live. Your people will be my people, and your God will be my God. Wherever you die, I will die, and there I will be buried. May the L*ORD *punish me severely if I allow anything but death to separate us!"'*

God also says: 'Don't ask me to leave you, because I won't.'
God also says: 'Wherever you are, I'm there too.'
God also says: 'What matters to you, matters to me.'
And God takes it a step further, as only he can:
'Not even death will separate us. I won't allow it.'
And he sent Jesus.
Our Boaz.
Our guardian-redeemer.

Day 30

Galatians 4:5 (<small>NLT</small>):
'God sent him [Jesus] to buy freedom for us'.

Father God,

Thank you that you never leave me.
Whatever my empty places look like,
you come.
And you fill them, bringing
your peace and love.
In your love, you bring me back,
again and again.
Every time I lose my way.
Thank you that I am safe with you.

Amen

Ruth's Reminder

I'm safe with God

My response:

Hosea 2:23 (NLT):

'And to those I called "Not my people,"
I will say, "Now you are my people."
And they will reply, "You are our God!"'

Romans 8:38,39 (NLT):

'And I am convinced that nothing can ever separate us
from God's love. Neither death nor life, neither angels
nor demons, neither our fears for today nor our worries
about tomorrow – not even the powers of hell can sep-
arate us from God's love. No power in the sky above or
in the earth below – indeed, nothing in all creation will
ever be able to separate us from the love of God that is
revealed in Christ Jesus our Lord.'

NOTES

[1] https://www.biblestudytools.com/lexicons/hebrew/kjv/leb.
html#Legend (accessed 27.8.20).
[2] https://www.biblestudytools.com/lexicons/hebrew/kjv/yare.
html (accessed 26.8.20).

Authentic

We trust you enjoyed reading this book
from Authentic. If you want to be
informed of any new titles from this author
and other releases you can sign up to the
Authentic newsletter by scanning below:

Online:
authenticmedia.co.uk

Follow us: